Palgrave Studies in Austrian Economics

This series provides insights to the key debates within Austrian economics. It presents advanced research that links current discussions on Austrian economics within its rich and influential intellectual tradition. Bringing together books from the leading researchers in this field, the varied the series aims to define the current scope of research within Austrian economics and shape directions of future analysis, with entries that offer both a foundation to the topic for those new to Austrian economics and fresh insights and debates for those who are well versed on the topic.

Renaud Fillieule

The Austrian School of Economics

Concepts and Theories

palgrave
macmillan

Renaud Fillieule
Faculty of Economics, Social Sciences,
Geography and Planning
University of Lille
Lille, France

ISSN 3005-0464 ISSN 3005-0472 (electronic)
Palgrave Studies in Austrian Economics
ISBN 978-3-031-83413-4 ISBN 978-3-031-83414-1 (eBook)
https://doi.org/10.1007/978-3-031-83414-1

This Palgrave Macmillan imprint is published by the registered company Springer Nature Switzerland AG.
The registered company address is: Gewerbestrasse 11, 6330 Cham, Switzerland

Preface

This book offers a comprehensive overview of the concepts and theories of the Austrian School, one of the leading heterodox schools of thought in economics. Established in the late nineteenth century during the Neoclassical revolution and further developed by some of the most influential theorists of the twentieth century, the Austrian School is currently experiencing a resurgence, in part due to its analysis of business cycles and its critique of government policies aimed at addressing recessions.

The book demonstrates that the Austrian School represents a distinct paradigm, employing its unique concepts and theoretical framework to address all major areas of economic analysis. These range from the concept of value and the formation of market prices to the nature of the competitive process, the laws of production, monetary phenomena, business cycles, and the impact of state intervention. The Austrian theorists also offer one of the strongest defenses of the market economy.

This volume will appeal to students of economics and social sciences who are looking for a coherent, rigorous, synthetic, and accessible exploration of economic analysis, grounded in verbal reasoning rather than mathematical formalism.

La Madeleine, France — Renaud Fillieule

Acknowledgments

The author would like to first thank his colleagues at the University of Lille, Laurent Cordonnier and Franck Van de Velde, for encouraging him to write this book and for publishing the original edition as part of their series on heterodox economics, with the support of the CLERSÉ laboratory (UMR 8019). He extends special thanks to Laurent Carnis, Alain Fillieule, Guido Hülsmann, and Pierre-Édouard Visse for their valuable feedback on the manuscript. Further appreciation goes to Philipp Bagus and David Howden for their immediate interest in including the book in their new Palgrave Studies in Austrian Economics series. Finally, the author is grateful to Wyndham Hacket Pain, Senior Editor at Palgrave Macmillan, and Christèle Meulin, Executive Director at Presses Universitaires du Septentrion, for overseeing the publication process.

Competing Interests The author has no competing interests to declare that are relevant to the content of this manuscript.

Contents

About the Author

Renaud Fillieule is Professor of Sociology at the University of Lille, France, and a member of the CLERSÉ research laboratory (UMR 8019). Educated as an engineer at École Centrale de Lyon, he later pursued studies in philosophy, sociology, and economics at the Sorbonne Universities. His sociology dissertation, completed in 1994, dealt with the question of rationality in the social sciences. In 2006, he earned his habilitation to direct research with a study on the economic sociology of prices. His current research centers on the Austrian School of Economics, particularly in the areas of the formalization of the structure of production and the theory of the interest rate.

List of Figures

CHAPTER 1

Introduction

Abstract The Austrian School of Economics, founded by Carl Menger in the late nineteenth century, develops a distinctive approach to economic analysis compared to mainstream Neoclassical paradigms. Its key contributors include Menger, Böhm-Bawerk, Mises, Hayek, Rothbard, and Kirzner.

Keyword Austrian School of Economics

What are the fundamental principles and key developments in economic analysis? This book aims to present the Austrian School's response to this question. This school was founded by Carl Menger in the late nineteenth century, who developed a theory of goods, a theory of value, and a theory of exchange. Menger's successors expanded these foundations with theories of capital, interest, entrepreneurship, money, business cycles, state intervention, and collectivism.

This book is intended for readers seeking to discover or deepen their understanding of Austrian economic theories. It can also serve as an introduction to more comprehensive and detailed works, such as Rothbard (1962) and Mises (1998 [1949]). More broadly, it will appeal to anyone looking for a concise, rigorous, yet non-mathematical presentation of economic science.

R. Fillieule, *The Austrian School of Economics*, Palgrave Studies in Austrian Economics,
https://doi.org/10.1007/978-3-031-83414-1_1

1.1 The Austrian School: A Distinct Paradigm

The Austrian School represents a paradigm in its own right, distinct from the standard Neoclassical paradigm that dominates modern economic teaching. This difference is evident from the outset in its theory of value. Key concepts such as those of structure of production, imputation, and specificity and convertibility of production factors are absent from standard textbooks. Austrian price theory emphasizes adaptation to dynamic shocks through capital reallocation between branches and the elimination of entrepreneurial profits and losses, diverging significantly from standard general equilibrium and partial equilibrium models.

The Austrian critique of orthodox views on competition—particularly perfect and monopolistic competition—centers on their failure to capture the true nature of the competitive process in a market economy. Instead, Austrians conceive of competition as rivalry, acknowledging the radical uncertainty of the future and the entrepreneurial role in discovering and exploiting profit opportunities.

In areas commonly referred to as macroeconomics and pertaining to capital structure, interest rates, money, and business cycles, the Austrian approach differs sharply from mainstream thought. Again, key Austrian notions—structure of production, roundaboutness, capitalization, and gross domestic output (much larger than the usual "gross domestic product")—are entirely missing from conventional presentations. The Austrian School's critique of Keynesian economics is particularly direct, rejecting the "paradox of saving" and opposing inflationary monetary policies.

The purpose of this book is not to exhaustively analyze the points of contention between the Austrian School and other economic paradigms, although some will be touched upon. Rather, it seeks to offer *a synthetic overview of the fundamental economic concepts and theories of the Austrian School*, which emerged from the joint efforts of successive generations of brilliant and influential economists. This book provides a compact yet faithful account of this rich conceptual and theoretical tradition.

1.2 Main Economists of the Austrian School (up to the 1970s)

The Austrian paradigm was gradually constructed through the contributions of successive economists who developed the core elements of a comprehensive system of economic analysis. The main figures include four

Austrian-born authors: Carl Menger, Eugen von Böhm-Bawerk, Ludwig von Mises, and Friedrich von Hayek. Other notable contributors include Friedrich von Wieser, Frank Fetter, Murray Rothbard, and Israel Kirzner. Additionally, John Bates Clark and Frank Knight, though part of the American School, had a strong influence on the Austrian paradigm.

- Carl Menger (1840–1921): theory of goods, theory of value, theory of exchange, theory of auction prices (*Grundsätze der Volkswirtschaftslehre—Principles of Economics*, 1976 [1871])
- Friedrich von Wieser (1851–1926): theory of the value of convertible factors of production (*Der natürliche Werth—Natural Value*, 1893 [1889])
- Eugen von Böhm-Bawerk (1851–1914): theory of capital (detour of production), reinterpretation of the "law of costs," theory of time preference, theory of interest (*Positive Theorie des Kapitales—Positive Theory of Capital*, 1959 [1889])
- [John Bates Clark (1847–1938): theory of dynamic changes, notion of functional distribution (*The Distribution of Wealth*, 1899)]
- Frank Fetter (1863–1949): capitalization theory (*Economic Principles*, 1915)
- Ludwig von Mises (1881–1973): theory of money, theory of credit, theory of business cycle, theory of economic calculation, theory of collectivism, theory of state interventionism (*Theorie des Geldes und der Umlaufsmittel—Theory of Money and Credit*, 1980 [1912]; *Die Gemeinwirtschaft—Socialism*, 1981a [1922]; *Human Action*, 1998 [1949])
- [Frank Knight (1885–1972): entrepreneurial profit theory (*Risk, Uncertainty, and Profit*, 1921)]
- Friedrich von Hayek (1899–1992): macroeconomics of the structure of production (Hayekian triangles), critique of collectivism (complexity argument), theory of dynamic competition (*Prices and Production*, 1931; *The Pure Theory of Capital*, 1941; *Individualism and Economic Order*, 1948)
- Murray Rothbard (1926–1995): critique of monopoly pricing theory, theory of taxes and state spending (*Man, Economy, and State*, 1962; *Power and Market*, 1977 [1970])
- Israel Kirzner (born in 1930): theory of entrepreneurial competition (*Competition and Entrepreneurship*, 1973)

Although associated with the Austrian School, Joseph Schumpeter (1883–1950) is not listed among the core figures because his theories diverged significantly from the traditional Austrian framework developed by Menger, Böhm-Bawerk, Mises, and Hayek.

Central to this framework is Ludwig von Mises, whose 1949 treatise *Human Action* synthesizes the Austrian School's theoretical and epistemological principles while rejecting mathematical economics as developed by the Lausanne School of Walras and Pareto. Although many contemporary economists continue to explore and expand upon the Austrian tradition (Skousen, 1990; Reisman, 1996; Huerta de Soto, 2006 [1998]; Salerno, 2010; Hülsmann, 2024, etc.), this book generally focuses on the "classical" contributors who laid the foundation of the school.

It is important to note that the following chapters exclusively deal with questions of economic *theory*. Major works on the methodology and epistemology of social science, such as those by Menger (1985 [1883]), Mises (1962, 1981b [1933], 1998 [1949], 2007 [1957]), Hayek (1952, 1967 [1964], 1978 [1974]), and others, will be omitted. Similarly, the numerous texts and works of political philosophy that defend and illustrate liberalism and libertarianism fall outside the scope of this book (see, e.g., Mises, 2005 [1927]; Hayek, 1960; Rothbard, 1998 [1982]).

References

Clark, J. B. (1899). *The Distribution of Wealth. A Theory of Wages, Interest, and Profits*. Macmillan.

Fetter, F. (1915). *Economic Principles*. Century.

Hayek, F. A. (1931). *Prices and Production*. George Routledge & Sons.

Hayek, F. A. (1941). *The Pure Theory of Capital*. The University of Chicago Press.

Hayek, F. A. (1948). *Individualism and Economic Order*. The University of Chicago Press.

Hayek, F. A. (1952). *The Counter-Revolution of Science. Studies on the Abuse of Reason*. The Free Press.

Hayek, F. A. (1960). *The Constitution of Liberty*. Routledge & Kegan Paul.

Hayek, F. A. (1967 [1964]). The Theory of Complex Phenomena. In F. A. Hayek (Ed.), *Studies in Philosophy, Politics and Economics* (pp. 22–42). Routledge & Kegan Paul.

Hayek, F. A. (1978 [1974]). The Pretence of Knowledge. In F. A. Hayek (Ed.), *New Studies in Philosophy, Politics, Economics and the History of Ideas* (pp. 23–34). Routledge & Kegan Paul.

Huerta de Soto, J. (2006 [1998]). *Money, Bank Credit, and Economic Cycles.* Ludwig von Mises Institute.

Hülsmann, J. G. (2024). *Abundance, Generosity, and the State. An Inquiry into Economic Principles.* Ludwig von Mises Institute.

Kirzner, I. M. (1973). *Competition and Entrepreneurship.* The University of Chicago Press.

Knight, F. H. (1921). *Risk, Uncertainty, and Profit.* Houghton Mifflin Company.

Menger, C. (1976 [1871]). *Principles of Economics.* New York University Press.

Menger, C. (1985 [1883]). *Investigations Into the Method of the Social Sciences.* New York University Press.

Reisman, G. (1996). *Capitalism. A Treatise on Economics.* Jameson Books.

Rothbard, M. N. (1962). *Man, Economy, and State. A Treatise on Economic Principles.* D. Van Nostrand.

Rothbard, M. N. (1977 [1970]). *Power and Market. Government and the Economy.* Sheed Andrews and McMeel.

Rothbard, M. N. (1998 [1982]). *The Ethics of Liberty.* New York University Press.

Salerno, J. T. (2010). *Money, Sound and Unsound.* Ludwig von Mises Institute.

Skousen, M. (1990). *The Structure of Production.* New York University Press.

von Böhm-Bawerk, E. (1959 [1889]). *Positive Theory of Capital.* Libertarian Press.

von Mises, L. (1962). *The Ultimate Foundation of Economic Science. An Essay on Method.* D. Van Nostrand.

von Mises, L. (1980 [1912]). *The Theory of Money and Credit.* LibertyClassics.

von Mises, L. (1981a [1922]). *Socialism. An Economic and Sociological Analysis.* LibertyClassics.

von Mises, L. (1981b [1933]). *Epistemological Problems of Economics.* New York University Press.

von Mises, L. (1998 [1949]). *Human Action. A Treatise on Economics.* Ludwig von Mises Institute.

von Mises, L. (2005 [1927]). *Liberalism. The Classical Tradition.* Liberty Fund.

von Mises, L. (2007 [1957]). *Theory and History. An Interpretation of Social and Economic Evolution.* Ludwig von Mises Institute.

von Wieser, F. (1893 [1889]). *Natural Value.* Macmillan.

CHAPTER 2

Goods and Value

Abstract Carl Menger explores what makes something a "good" for an individual and identifies four conditions: a human need, the ability of the thing to satisfy that need, knowledge of its utility, and control over it. The chapter then examines what is the "value" of a good for an individual. It emphasizes that value is subjective, arising from individual needs and perceptions at specific moments, not from inherent qualities of the goods themselves. Key ideas include the law of marginal utility, the imputation principle, and the role of time and opportunity costs in valuation.

Keywords Economic goods • Subjective value • Marginal utility • Imputation

The foundations of Austrian economic theory were established by its originator, Carl Menger (1976 [1871]), in response to two fundamental questions. First, under what conditions does something become useful to an individual, or in other words, when can it be considered a *good* for that person? Second, how can we explain why a good has *value* to an individual, and how do we determine the level of this value? Menger's answers to these questions form the basis of his theory of goods and his theory of value, the two core pillars of Austrian economics.

R. Fillieule, *The Austrian School of Economics*, Palgrave Studies in Austrian Economics,
https://doi.org/10.1007/978-3-031-83414-1_2

2.1 The Theory of Goods

2.1.1 The Four Prerequisites for a Good

Menger's theory of goods begins with the concept of *human need.* If a person moves from a state of need to one of satisfaction, it means that some "thing" has played a role in meeting that need. This thing is then considered *useful.* Furthermore, if the individual has consciously used it to meet the need, that thing becomes a *good.* According to Menger, four conditions must be present for something to be classified as a good:

1. A human need;
2. The ability of the thing to satisfy that need;
3. Knowledge of this ability;
4. Control over the thing, allowing it to be used to meet the need.

2.1.2 Goods and Subjectivity

New needs, new knowledge, or new methods of control can transform previously non-useful things into goods. For instance, an oil deposit becomes a good once its usefulness is understood and the technology to extract it becomes available. Thus, the status of a thing as a good is not an "inherent" property of the thing itself but is instead defined by the *relationship* between the individual and the thing. Menger illustrates this with an example: if the desire for tobacco suddenly vanished, all items related solely to satisfying the need for tobacco—such as cigarette packs, stored tobacco stocks, harvested leaves, and seeds—would immediately lose their status as goods. However, items that could serve other purposes, such as farmland repurposed for other crops, would retain their character as goods.

Böhm-Bawerk (1962 [1881]) characterizes goods through the lens of *subjectivity.* It is the individual's knowledge and perception of their needs that determine whether something is considered a good. Even the objective qualities of a good are only understood through the subjective perspective of the individual. A thing is not a good in an absolute sense, but rather for a specific individual, at a certain time, and in a particular situation.

2.1.3 *Services*

Menger defines goods as "things" but emphasizes that they are not necessarily material objects. One type of immaterial good is labor services. Some consumer goods, such as a doctor's diagnosis, a musician's concert, or a lawyer's plea, are also considered services. Unlike the common modern distinction between goods and services, the Austrian economists categorize them both under the broader term "goods," distinguishing only between "material goods" and "services" (immaterial goods).

2.1.4 *Higher-Order Goods and Stages of Production*

Menger classifies goods into two main categories: those that *directly* satisfy needs, known as consumer goods, and those that *indirectly* satisfy needs, referred to as factors of production. He also introduces a refined classification based on a good's proximity to final consumption. For example, a baguette ready for consumption is a first-order good (a consumer good), while the flour used to bake it is a second-order good. The wheat used to produce the flour is a third-order good, and the seeds for growing the wheat are a fourth-order good, and so on.

These different orders of goods are arranged vertically (see Fig. 2.1), with goods closest to consumption at the bottom (downstream) and those

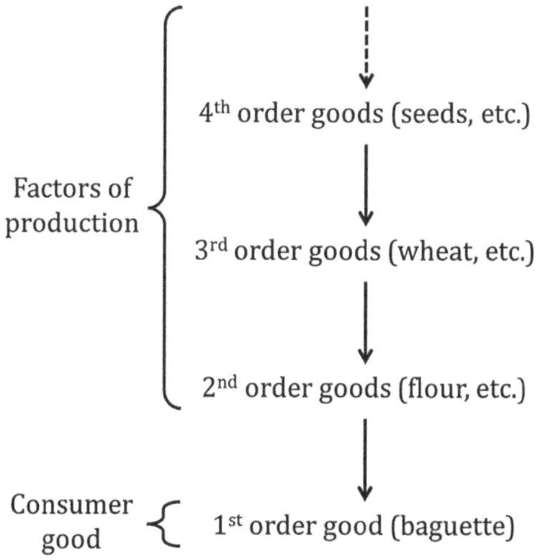

Fig. 2.1 Higher and lower orders of goods

furthest from consumption at the top (upstream). Goods of order two and higher are factors of production and may belong to either "lower" stages (closer to final consumption) or "higher" stages (further from final consumption). The *structure of production* is a complex system of multiple and interconnected stages that ultimately result in all consumer goods.

2.1.5 Goods: Complementary Versus Substitutable, Convertible Versus Specific

For a higher-order good to satisfy needs, the economic actor must possess *other* essential goods, which Menger refers to as "complementary goods," necessary to complete the production process. For example, if an individual has wheat but lacks the complementary goods required to transform it into bread, the wheat is not a good for that person (assuming they cannot use it in any other way).

Menger focuses on the causal relationship between complementary goods of different orders (1976 [1871], p. 63). He formulates the principle that the status of higher-order goods as goods is derived from the status of the lower-order goods they help produce. In simpler terms, a higher-order good is considered a good because the things it helps create are goods. For instance, bread is a good, so the flour used to produce it is also a good; in turn, because flour is a good, wheat is a good, and so on upward throughout the production process. This principle, where the status of a good is passed from lower to higher stages, applies to goods themselves the concept of *imputation* (see Sect. 2.3.1).

While Menger does not explicitly analyze beyond complementarity, it is easy to extend his ideas to later distinctions between complementary and substitutable goods, and between convertible and specific goods. Imagine a higher-order good *A*, which requires a complementary good *B*. If *B* becomes unavailable, does *A* lose its status as a good? Not necessarily. If a *substitute* for *B*, say good *C*, is available, then *A* can retain its status as a good. If no substitute is available, *A* can still be a good, provided it is *convertible*—meaning it can be used in another production process where all complementary goods are available. However, if *A* is *specific*—only usable in one production process—and its complementary good *B* has no substitute, *A* loses its status as a good if *B* goes missing.

2.1.6 "Non-Economic" Goods

Menger distinguishes between "economic" goods, which are scarce relative to needs and must be economized, and "non-economic" goods, which exist in overabundance. A classic example of a "non-economic" or free good is the air we breathe. Air satisfies the vital need for respiration and is available in quantities that far exceed our requirements (except in rare circumstances). However, Mises argued that air is *not* a "good" because its use does not require any conscious action on the part of individuals (1998 [1949], p. 93). According to him, when something benefits a person without requiring intentional effort, it should not be defined as a good but rather as a *general condition of human welfare*.

Mises' objection is not merely a matter of terminology, where "general condition of human welfare" is synonymous with "non-economic good." Menger's reasoning is based on the concept of *need*, while Mises' argument centers on the notion of *action*. While every action aims to satisfy a need, not every need is satisfied through action, as seen in the case of breathing. An action implies that the actor has a specific goal and consciously uses certain *means* to achieve it. In this framework, a good is simply a means employed in an action, and a means must be scarce; if it were superabundant, it would not require any action to obtain it (Rothbard, 1962, p. 4).

2.1.7 "Imaginary" Goods

Menger distinguishes between "real" goods and "imaginary" goods. Imaginary goods are those for which the causal relationship outlined in condition (2) above ("The ability of the thing to satisfy that need") is objectively false. In other words, people *believe* that the thing is able to satisfy their need, but this belief is mistaken. A typical example would be ancient medicinal potions thought to cure certain illnesses, though they are actually ineffective. Menger argues that, as civilization advances and people gain more knowledge of the world, the number of "real" goods increases, while the number of "imaginary" goods decreases.

However, is this distinction relevant to economic analysis? While it is critical for natural sciences, which seek to uncover the true causes of phenomena, it may not be as important for economists studying the concept of a good. For the economist, it does not matter whether the causal relationship is objectively true or not. As long as people believe that a thing can satisfy their needs, it functions as a good for them—even if others, who do not share that belief, would not consider it a good (Mises, 1998 [1949], p. 93). Thus, conditions (2) and (3) can be combined into a new condition (2′), which better accounts for the role of subjectivity in defining a good:

- (2′) The belief in the thing's causal ability to satisfy the need.

2.1.8 Are Property Rights and "Relationships" Goods?

Property rights represent immaterial relationships between economic actors and goods. Böhm-Bawerk (1962 [1881]) explored whether these rights themselves could be considered goods and concluded they are not. A property right simply reinforces the likelihood of controlling a good, through the protection provided by the State's police and justice systems. The role of the State is to ensure that property is held by its rightful owners or returned to them if it has been stolen. However, the right to property is not a good in itself because as such it does not satisfy any needs. Only possessed and controlled goods can fulfill a need. If a person's good is stolen, lost, or destroyed, their property right may remain intact, but it no longer satisfies their need (since condition (4) is no longer met).

Böhm-Bawerk further argues that if property rights were considered goods, then the owner of a good would possess two goods: the good itself and the right to it. This would result in an unjustifiable doubling of the number of goods.

Menger, on the other hand, includes what he calls "relationships" in the category of goods. Examples he provides include businesses, customer bases, monopolies, copyrights, patents, and exclusive commercial privileges, as well as personal relationships like family and friendships. However, applying Böhm-Bawerk's logic, we must conclude that these relationships are not goods. For instance, while a friend's support during a difficult time may be considered a good, it is the act of support—the service itself—that qualifies as a good, not the friendship. Similarly, copyright is not a good; it is the income it generates (if any) that counts as a good. Menger justifies his claim by arguing that businesses, client bases, and other such "relationships" can be bought and sold, and therefore must be goods. However, by Menger's own definition, since these "relationships" as such do not satisfy needs they should not be classified as goods.

2.1.9 *Time*

As will be seen in its theories of production and interest, the Austrian School places significant emphasis on the role of time in human action. Mises discusses the scarcity of time and the necessity of economizing it (1998 [1949], p. 101), while Rothbard goes so far as to consider time itself a good, as it is an indispensable resource for any action (1962, p. 11). In contrast, Hülsmann (2024, p. 54) considers time as a free "general condition of welfare," a dimension of any action, that does not meet Menger's criteria for a good.

2.1.10 *Critique of the "Public Good" Concept*

Mainstream Neoclassical economics, especially since Samuelson's work (1954), has developed the concept of "public goods" or "collective goods." A good is classified as "public" if one person's consumption of it does not reduce its availability to others (non-rivalry), and if it is impossible to exclude anyone from its consumption (non-exclusion). This is in contrast to the classic "private good," which is both rivalrous and exclusive.

Rothbard (1962, pp. 884–885) develops a critique of the notion of public goods from an Austrian perspective. *National defense*, typically cited as the most obvious example of a public good, is provided by a nation's military forces. However, Rothbard questions whether military forces are truly a good for citizens based on Menger's condition (1), which requires a human need to be satisfied. What need does national defense satisfy? One could argue it meets the need for living in a peaceful country, protected from external aggression. But if this need is not recognized by the population, then condition (1) is not satisfied, and the armed forces are not a good in that context.

Even if we assume that the population unanimously desires peace, we must also evaluate condition (2′), which requires a belief in the causal effectiveness of military forces to satisfy this need. Some pacifists may argue that military forces provoke other countries rather than deter them, potentially triggering conflict rather than preventing it. For such individuals, condition (2′) is not met, and national defense would not be considered a good.

Rothbard highlights another issue: military resources are not evenly distributed across a country, meaning some areas are better protected than others. This violates both the principle of non-rivalry and non-exclusion, further challenging the idea of a "public" good. In light of these arguments, the very existence of public goods is called into question.

2.2 Subjective Value

2.2.1 *Definition and Origin of Value*

Menger defines the value of a good as the *importance* an individual attributes to it based on its ability to directly or indirectly satisfy their needs. "Non-economic" goods—those available in overabundant quantities—have no value. Whether or not one possesses a unit of such a good has no impact on their ability to meet their needs, as other identical units are effortlessly and instantaneously available. Therefore, a unit of a non-economic good holds no importance and is essentially worthless to the individual. For example, a breath of air under normal conditions has no value because, if deprived of one, the individual can easily meet the need to breathe from the surrounding abundance of air. In contrast, only "economic" goods, those whose supply is limited relative to demand, possess value. In other words, *scarcity* is a prerequisite for value.

If we follow Mises in rejecting the notion of "non-economic" goods and instead assert that a good is inherently scarce (and thus economized), then we can simply state that all goods have value. If something has no value, it is overabundant or useless, and therefore is not a good.

2.2.2 *Value and Subjectivity*

Menger emphasizes that value is not inherent in goods but is determined by an individual's relationship to them. A good that has immense value to an individual in one context (such as a sack of water in the desert) may hold little value in another (the same amount of water near a plentiful spring). As Böhm-Bawerk points out, this type of value is *subjective*, determined by the individual's specific hierarchy of needs and their available resources at a particular time. Two individuals in similar situations may assess the same good very differently, depending on their personal preferences. For a given individual, if tastes or circumstances change, the value attributed to goods will also shift. For instance, as people grow into adulthood, the value they place on childhood toys tends to disappear, while things that once held no value to them may now become valuable.

Böhm-Bawerk notes that "value" can have various meanings. He distinguishes between subjective value and objective value. When we say a good is "worth" a certain amount of money, we refer to its *objective* value, which is simply its price. In this discussion, unless otherwise specified, "value" refers to subjective value.

2.2.3 *The Scale of Values*

The values an individual assigns to different goods form a hierarchy, with some goods considered more valuable than others. This hierarchy can change depending on the situation or moment. According to Menger, the hierarchy of values follows a simple principle: the more crucial a need is to an individual in a given context, the higher its value. Individuals thus assign value to their needs and then transfer—or *impute*—it to goods based on their importance in fulfilling these needs.

This hierarchy of values is based on *concrete*, specific needs, not abstract categories. For example, although the category "food" may generally be ranked higher than "entertainment" for biological survival, an individual whose immediate food needs are met may place more importance on fulfilling a need for entertainment over additional food. In such a case, the individual would assign more value to attending a show than to an extra portion of food.

2.2.4 *Resolving the "Paradox of Value"*

The more important or useful a good is for an individual, the more value it possesses. This core principle of subjective valuation seems to conflict with the famous "paradox of value" highlighted by Classical economists (Smith, 1976 [1776], pp. 32–33). If a good's value increases with its importance or usefulness, why is water—essential for survival—so cheap, while diamonds, which fulfill no vital need, are so expensive? After all, it is far more important to quench one's thirst than to own a piece of diamond jewelry. If value came from importance for the individual, water should be much more valuable than diamonds, but it is not. Unable to solve this paradox, Smith rejected the idea that utility explains value and developed instead a labor theory of value (according to which the value of a commodity is proportional to the quantity of labor that went into producing it).

Menger responds that, under normal conditions, water is abundantly available. The value of the water in a glass is low because, even if deprived of it, an individual would still have access to large quantities of water to satisfy a need to drink. The water in the glass holds little significance or usefulness to the individual, as it can be quickly and almost without cost replaced at the faucet. Consequently, it has minimal value. In contrast, diamonds are scarce, and losing one would prevent the individual from satisfying far more significant needs, given their limited availability and high demand—hence their great value. Therefore, rather than contradicting the principle of subjective valuation, this example actually reinforces it. When the situation is correctly analyzed, the paradox vanishes, eliminating the need for Smith's solution based on the labor theory of value.

2.2.5 Unit and Stock

The paradox of value arises from confusion between the concepts of a "unit" of a good and the total "stock" of a good. When people think, "water is much more useful than diamonds and should therefore be much more valuable," they are implicitly reasoning in terms of the entire stock of water available to humanity. It is true that if an individual had to choose between all the drinking water (the entire water stock) and all the diamonds (the entire diamond stock), they would choose the water, attributing more value to it than to the diamonds.

However, individuals do not choose between the total stocks of these goods but rather between specific, *concrete units*. As Menger explains, people make choices here about very small quantities relative to the total stock. To correctly analyze how individuals assign value, we must focus on the units of goods relevant to the concrete decisions they are making. What is the value of a particular unit of a good to a specific individual at a given moment? Why is someone willing to exchange a unit of one good for a unit of another? Why does someone allocate a unit of a higher-order good to one production line rather than another? The unit, not the entire stock, is the key element in understanding the valuation process.

The concept of a unit, like the notions of goods and value, is subjective (Rothbard, 1956, p. 233). For instance, if four nails are needed to hang a picture, the relevant "unit" of the good consists of those four nails. The unit an individual considers depends on the specific goal aimed at and the action undertaken. This perspective leads Rothbard to criticize conventional mathematical models that treat a unit of a good as infinitesimally small, subject to differential calculus. Human actions are not about infinitesimally small things but about quantities that are discrete in the mathematical sense.

2.2.6 *The Law of Marginal Utility*

The concepts of "unit" and "stock" of a good lead to what Böhm-Bawerk considers the fundamental law of economic theory: the law of marginal utility. The term "marginal utility" was introduced by Wieser (1884) to refer to the subjective value of a single unit from a stock of goods (the original German term *Grenznutzen* was translated to "marginal utility" in 1889). Let us consider an individual who possesses a stock of goods:

- The units within this stock are, by definition, *identical* to the individual; otherwise, they would be considered different goods.
- Since they are interchangeable, each unit holds the *same* subjective value for the individual.
- "Marginal utility" refers to the subjective value of *one unit* of this stock (if the stock is reduced to just one unit, marginal utility equals the total utility).
- The *law of marginal utility* states that the marginal utility of a good is the value of the *least important need* that the individual intends to satisfy with one unit of the available stock.
- This is a *praxeological* law, as defined by Mises (1998 [1949], p. 124): it is not based on observation, experimentation, or testing, but is a formal, a priori law of human action—necessarily true by the very definitions of the terms used.

Böhm-Bawerk (1959b [1889], p. 143) explains this law using Menger's example of an isolated farmer with five sacks of wheat after the harvest. The farmer allocates the wheat to different needs in order of importance:

1. The first sack ensures his minimum subsistence until the next harvest.
2. The second sack improves his meals, keeping him healthy.
3. The third sack feeds poultry, providing him with meat for more varied meals.
4. The fourth sack is used to produce alcoholic beverages through distillation.
5. The fifth sack is for feeding his pets.

Since all five sacks are identical and interchangeable, they hold the same value for the farmer. But what is this value? To determine it, we ask which satisfaction the farmer would sacrifice if one of the sacks were lost. Clearly, he would not give up food. Instead, he would forego the least important need—in this case, feeding his pets. Thus, the marginal utility of his wheat stock corresponds to the importance of the "last" need that the sacks satisfy.

2.2.7 Stock Variations and Marginal Utility

Menger and Böhm-Bawerk further illustrate the effect of stock changes by continuing the example of the isolated farmer. Suppose the farmer has only four sacks of wheat instead of five. In this case, the value of each sack increases because the last need satisfied with four sacks (producing beverages) is more important than the one satisfied with five sacks (feeding pets). Conversely, if the farmer had six sacks, the value of each sack would decrease, as the sixth sack would satisfy a less important need than feeding pets.

This demonstrates the principle: the more sacks the farmer has, the lower their subjective value; the fewer sacks he has, the higher their value. More generally, the law states that, everything else equal, if an individual's stock of a good increases, the marginal utility (utility of one unit) decreases; if the stock decreases, the marginal utility increases.

2.2.8 Significance of the Law

This law is fundamental because it accurately explains how people value goods and then express their demand for them. These demands, shaped by subjective preferences, interact with available supplies to establish the array of market prices. The Classical economics idea that commodity prices are determined by the amount of labor involved has been thoroughly refuted. Price theory is now founded on a solid principle of valuation rooted in subjectivity and marginal utility (see Sect. 3.2). A value judgment results from a mental process and it cannot be reduced to, or equated with, an objective quantity of labor or of anything else.

2.2.9 Measuring Values?

In explaining his theory, Menger assumes that values can be measured. He assigns a numerical value to each good that reflects its importance to the individual and *sums* these numbers to calculate the total value of the set of goods. Wieser (1893 [1889]) takes an even more simplistic approach, calculating the total value of a stock by multiplying the number of units in the stock by the marginal utility of one unit. Böhm-Bawerk (1959b

[1889], p. 147) also uses a similar method, adding up the values of each individual good in the stock to determine its total value. However, he criticizes Wieser's approach: the value of units diminishes as they are used to satisfy progressively less important needs, so the value of the stock is always higher than the sum of marginal utilities (since marginal utility represents the lowest value).

Mises (1980 [1912], pp. 51–55) definitively broke with this tradition, arguing that *subjective values are not measurable*. According to him, they form a ranking or hierarchy, allowing an individual to compare goods and determine which is more valuable, but not "by how much." In other words, values cannot be added together like lengths or quantities. Subjective values can only be ordered but not numerically calculated (Mises 1998 [1949], p. 122). This means it is impossible to derive the value of a stock from the sum of its units, or the value of a unit from the stock (unless the stock consists of just a single unit). Here, Mises aligned himself with Čuhel (1907), a non-Austrian economist, in a debate against Böhm-Bawerk on this issue (Hülsmann, 2007, p. 218). In the standard terminology, subjective values are *ordinal* rankings of preferences, not *cardinal* measurements.

2.2.10 Value and Indifference

Standard microeconomics represents economic choices through the concept of "indifference curves" (Pareto, 1981 [1909], pp. 168–169). An indifference curve represents a set of combinations of goods that provide the individual with the same level of satisfaction, meaning the individual is indifferent between them. However, Rothbard (1956, p. 236 ff) argues that indifference is incompatible with human action: to act is to make a choice. A person can always determine which of two goods is more valuable to them; the more valuable good is the one they would choose to keep if forced to give one up. Therefore, subjective values establish a *strict* order of preference between goods, and there is no room for indifference in the context of action.

2.2.11 Interpersonal Comparison of Values

Böhm-Bawerk concludes his analysis of the law of marginal utility by suggesting that a given quantity of a good holds greater value for a poor person than for a rich person. He reasons that the rich individual has access to a far larger stock of goods, so the gain or loss of one unit would matter less (low value), whereas, for the poor person, such a change would significantly affect their ability to meet their needs (high value).

However, in his influential work on economic analysis, Robbins (1932, pp. 122–124), who was strongly influenced by economists like Wicksteed and Mises, argues that this interpretation of the law of marginal utility is *scientifically flawed* (for the origins of these ideas in Čuhel, 1907, see Hülsmann, 2007, p. 219). The law of marginal utility applies strictly to a single individual: as their stock of a good increases (e.g., their amount of money), its marginal utility decreases, all else being equal. However, this law does not allow for comparing the values one individual attributes to a unit of money with those attributed by another. Therefore, one cannot conclude from this law that taxing the rich to subsidize the poor will increase overall societal satisfaction. Such decisions must be based on ethical principles and cannot be scientifically justified by the law of marginal utility.

2.2.12 Preference for the Present (Time Preference)

The relationship between subjective values and time serves as a foundation for Austrian theories of production, capital, and interest. Menger observed that, generally, present satisfaction is more valuable to individuals than an equivalent satisfaction in the future (1976 [1871], pp. 153–154). He attributes this preference for the present to emotional reasons that can seem tautological: the fear of running out of goods is stronger for the immediate future than for distant times. However, this is the very phenomenon that needs explanation. Menger also provides a more rational justification: the satisfaction of future needs depends on the prior satisfaction of present ones. Over-sacrificing present needs may jeopardize future well-being. In other words, we must survive today and in the near future to enjoy satisfaction later. From this, we can infer that, in general, a present good is more valuable than the same good in the future.

Böhm-Bawerk (1959b [1889], p. 259) formalized this principle as the basis of his theory of interest, offering three reasons for the preference for the present:

1. *Present need* versus *future need*: Individuals who are worse off in the present than they expect to be in the future naturally attribute more value to present goods. On the other hand, those who are better off in the present can transfer resources to the future, so they also generally prefer present goods to future ones.

2. *Uncertainty of the future and impulsivity*: People tend to underestimate future satisfaction due to uncertainty—there is no guarantee they will live to enjoy future goods—and a lack of self-discipline, as the temptation to indulge in present consumption can outweigh future rewards. This explanation is shared by Wieser (1893 [1889], p. 17), who highlights the conflict between impulse and reason.
3. *Production advantage of present goods*: Having a factor of production in the present is always preferable because it can be used to increase the quantity of future consumer goods (see Sect. 5.1.8).

Fetter (1915, p. 240), one of Böhm-Bawerk's main successors on this topic, also emphasizes the uncertainty of the future as a key reason for the preference for present goods. He adds a biological explanation—though it might seem tautological—that "the impulse to seek immediate gratification is deeply rooted in human biology."

2.2.13 The Law of Time Preference

Mises was the first to articulate the law of time preference as a principle grounded in the pure logic of action (a praxeological principle), independent of any biological or psychological factors. He stated, "Other things being equal, satisfaction in a nearer period of the future is preferred to satisfaction in a more distant period" (1998 [1949], p. 480). His demonstration, employing reductio ad absurdum, proceeds as follows: let us envision a sequence of moments in time where the "all else being equal" condition holds true. If we assume that an individual opts not to consume a good at the first moment, then there is no reason—given that all else is equal—for them to consume it at the second moment, nor at the third moment, and so on. This would imply that the individual would never consume the good, which is clearly absurd. Therefore, the individual must inevitably consume it at the first moment.

Mises' formulation of this law also helps explain its apparent exceptions. For instance, if an individual in winter prefers a stock of ice cubes available next summer to one that is immediately accessible, they are essentially comparing different goods. Ice is abundant in winter but scarce in summer, meaning the "all else being equal" condition is not satisfied in this case, and thus the (praxeological) law of time preference does not apply.

2.3 The Value of Factors of Production

2.3.1 *The Imputation Principle*

According to Menger, factors of production (higher-order goods) acquire their value based on the same principle as consumer goods, specifically, the importance an individual assigns to them in satisfying their needs. However, by definition, a higher-order good does not directly fulfill needs; rather, it contributes to a production process that results in lower-order goods, which ultimately leads to first-order goods (consumer goods).

A higher-order good can only possess value if the lower-order goods it helps produce also hold value. If the lower-order goods are deemed unimportant by the individual, then the higher-order good utilized to produce them cannot be valuable either. Furthermore, because the production process requires time, the individual must assign value to the higher-order good before the lower-order goods come into existence, necessitating the *anticipation* of their future value.

Menger logically concludes that the value of higher-order goods is "always and without exception determined by the prospective value of the goods of lower order in whose production they serve" (1976 [1871], p. 150). Böhm-Bawerk (1959b [1889], p. 170) illustrates this principle using the example of groups of production factors G_4, G_3, and G_2, which are employed in successive stages to produce a final good, Z (see Fig. 2.2).

If we assume that these groups of factors are irreplaceable (no substitutes) and specific (meaning they cannot be used to produce anything other than good Z), and if we disregard the duration of the production process (to avoid complications due to time preference), then all of these groups hold the *same value* for the individual as the produced good. By the principle of imputation, good Z imparts its value to factor group G_2: if the individual were deprived of G_2, they would lose the satisfaction associated with Z. Likewise, group G_2 conveys its value to factor group G_3 (if the individual were deprived of G_3, they would lose the satisfaction associated with G_2), and so on.

According to Menger's principle of imputation, a good *never* derives its value from the higher-order goods used to produce it, but instead from the lower-order goods that it helps to produce. This principle is one of the most significant and profound aspects of the Austrian interpretation of the Neoclassical revolution of the 1870s. It fundamentally contradicts all theories that attempt to explain the value of goods in terms of the factors

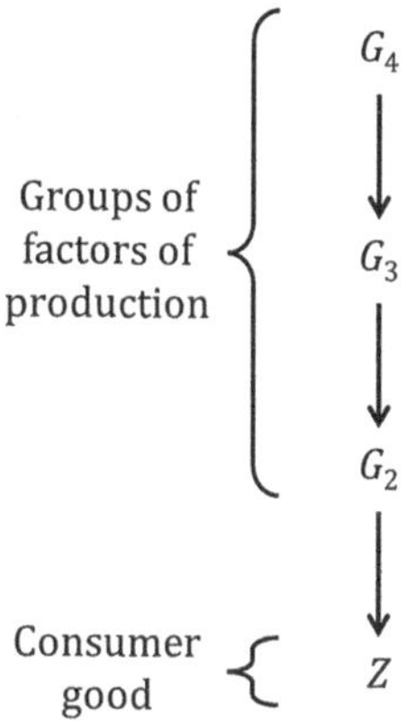

Fig. 2.2 The consumer good *Z* is produced by a succession of groups of production factors

utilized in their production. In particular, Menger argues that the efforts or sacrifices—often referred to as "real costs"—made to produce a good do not confer any value upon it. Instead, only a good's ability to satisfy (either directly or indirectly) future needs can account for its subjective valuation.

2.3.2 The Value of Complementary Factors

Given the necessary complementarity of production factors, we might wonder whether an individual can value these goods independently of one another. Menger answers affirmatively, stating that the value of a factor of production, like that of a consumer good, corresponds to the significance of the needs the individual would forgo if deprived of that factor. He observes that if the factor is replaceable, the individual can minimize the loss of satisfaction—though not eliminate it—by reorganizing production, which involves reallocating factors among different production lines.

To explore this further, we need to distinguish among various scenarios, depending on whether the factor is replaceable (by substitutes) or not, and whether its complementary factors are convertible.

Referring to Böhm-Bawerk's analysis (1959b [1889], pp. 162–163), which is more comprehensive and systematic than Menger's, let us consider three complementary factors: *A*, *B*, and *C*. The individual chooses to apply these factors to the production of a consumption good *Z*. For instance, we might envision that *A* represents a flashlight, *B* represents the battery for this flashlight, and *C* represents the labor required to insert the battery into its slot (see Fig. 2.3).

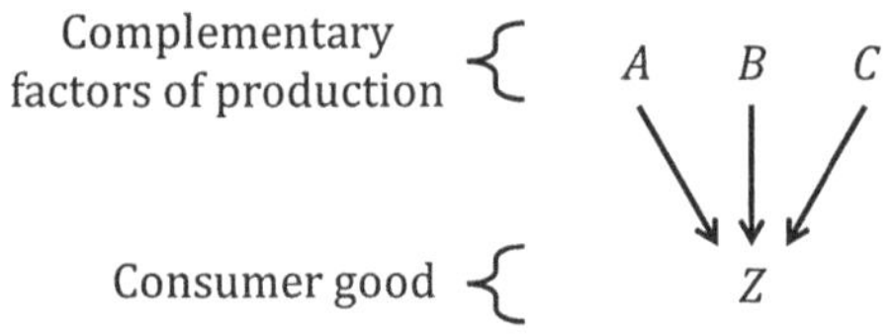

Fig. 2.3 Complementary factors *A*, *B*, and *C* produce the consumer good *Z*

To determine the value of good *A*, let us consider the scenario where the individual is deprived of it.

Case 1: *A* is *irreplaceable*, meaning no other good can substitute for it. If *B* and *C* are *specific* (i.e., they can only be used in this production process), then losing good *A* renders *B* and *C* completely valueless. As a result, the individual experiences the maximum loss of satisfaction, which corresponds to the loss of consumer good *Z* produced with the combination of *A*, *B*, and *C*. Conversely, if *B* and *C* are *convertible* (i.e., they can be used in other production processes), then the loss of good *A* does not render *B* and *C* valueless. Instead, they can be utilized in other processes, thereby reducing the loss of satisfaction compared to the first scenario.

Case 2: A is *replaceable*, meaning that the individual possesses another good, *D*, which can serve as a substitute. If *B* and *C* are *specific*, the individual has two options: (a) remove good *D* from the process it was initially assigned to and substitute it for *A* (changing the combination from *ABC* to *DBC*), or (b) retain good *D* for its original purpose, in which case *B* and *C* would become valueless. The individual will choose the option that minimizes the loss of satisfaction due to the loss of *A*. If *B* and *C* are *convertible*, the individual again has two options: (a) substitute good *D* for good *A*, or (b) make no substitution and reallocate goods *B* and *C* to other production processes. As before, the individual will select the option that results in the least reduction in satisfaction.

In situations where good *A* is replaceable and goods *B* or *C* are convertible, the individual benefits from more options to mitigate the loss of satisfaction resulting from the deprivation of *A*.

2.3.3 *Fixed or Variable Factor Proportions*

The preceding analysis has implicitly assumed *fixed proportions*: for example, combinations of goods *A*, *B*, and *C* produce good *Z* in specific ratios—2*A*, 2*B*, and 2*C* yield two units of *Z*, while 3*A*, 3*B*, and 3*C* yield three units of *Z*, and so on. Menger demonstrates that this reasoning can also apply to cases with ***variable proportions***, meaning that the consumption good *Z* can be produced using different combinations of *A*, *B*, and *C*.

For instance, if the individual has allocated 3*A*, 5*B*, and 4*C* to produce units of good *Z*, losing one unit of *A* allows for production to continue with a new combination of 2*A*, 5*B*, and 4*C*. Although the total production of the consumption good *Z* will decrease, the value of good *A*—the marginal utility of *A*—reflects the significance of the needs that the individual can no longer satisfy due to this reduction in production. More complex scenarios can be envisioned, especially if goods *B* and *C* are convertible.

2.3.4 Imputation and Convertible Factors

Menger articulated and demonstrated the principle of imputation, which explains how the value of factors is derived from the value of their products. However, it is Wieser (1884, 1893 [1889]) who deserves credit for illustrating how this principle applies in the crucial case of ***convertible*** factors. When a factor is specific—meaning it can only be used in one type of production process—it is straightforward to conclude that its value derives from the needs it satisfies. Böhm-Bawerk illustrates this point with the example of a Tokay vineyard: the vineyard's high value does not lead to the wine it produces being valuable; rather, it is the wine's high value that imparts value to the vineyard.

While the principle of imputation can be easily applied to specific assets, it becomes more complex with convertible assets. Consider a group of factors, *G*, which can be used to produce goods *X*, *Y*, and *Z*. Suppose the actor owns three units of *G* and decides to allocate them to the production of goods *X*, *Y*, and *Z*, as illustrated in Fig. 2.4.

Assuming that the value of good *Z* is the highest, we can assign it an arbitrary value of 12; good *X*, being the least valuable, receives a value of 5; and good *Y*, which falls in between, is assigned a value of 7. These numbers do not measure values; they simply indicate a ranking of preferences.

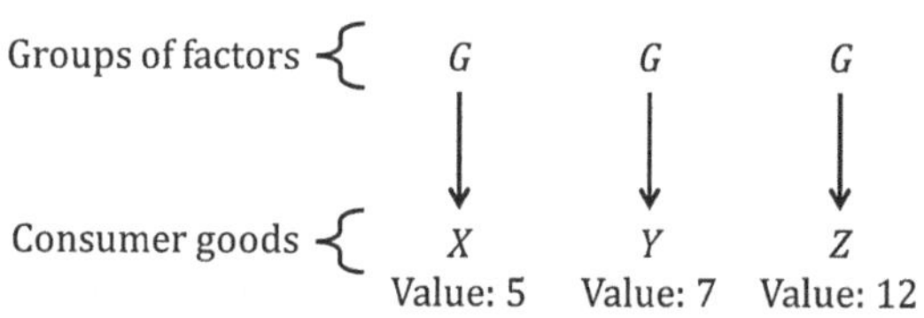

Fig. 2.4 Three groups of factors *G* are used to produce consumer goods *X*, *Y*, and *Z*

What is the value of one unit of factor *G*? It is 5 because if the individual loses this unit, they will choose to produce goods *Y* and *Z* using their two remaining units of factors, foregoing the lowest satisfaction, which is that derived from good *X* valued at 5.

If the value of product *Z* is 12 while the value of its factor *G* is only 5, does this contradict the principle of imputation? No, because the value of *Z* only reaches 12 once the *three* production processes ($G \rightarrow X$, $G \rightarrow Y$, $G \rightarrow Z$) are completed. At that point, the units of *G* no longer exist and therefore cannot hold any value. However, right after producing good *Z* and still having two units of *G* left, the value of *Z* equals 5. If the individual loses *Z*, they will utilize their remaining two units of *G* to produce *Y* and a new *Z*, meaning they would only sacrifice the value of *X*. Thus, the value of factor *G* (5) indeed matches the value of its product *Z* (5).

It may seem that factor *G* imposes its value of 5 on product *Z*, but analysis reveals that good *G* ultimately derives its value from the consumer goods it helps to produce, specifically good *X* in this case. Therefore, the principle of imputation holds true for convertible factors, as value imputation also occurs from products to their factors, albeit through a more indirect route. As Böhm-Bawerk states, convertible factors "reflect" the value they receive from their marginal product onto their other products (1959b [1889], p. 176).

2.3.5 Time Preference and Discounting

In all previous examples, the impact of time on valuation has been set aside for simplicity. Now, let us consider the inevitable passage of time between the use of production factors and the arrival of their product. When time is accounted for, the value of the factors can no longer be equal to the value of the product.

In Fig. 2.5, a recurring production process is illustrated where an individual chooses to use a factor, *F*, to produce a consumer good, *Z*, over a period of time *T*. At the start of any given period, say period 2, we see that the individual holds both goods *Z* and *F*. If the factor of time is ignored (instantaneous process), both *Z* and *F* would have the same value through imputation. However, with a specific time *T* between using the factor and obtaining the product, the consequences of losing either *Z* or *F* differ for the individual.

If the individual lacks *Z*, an immediate need cannot be satisfied, only a future need in the following period (period 3). If *F* is lacking, the current

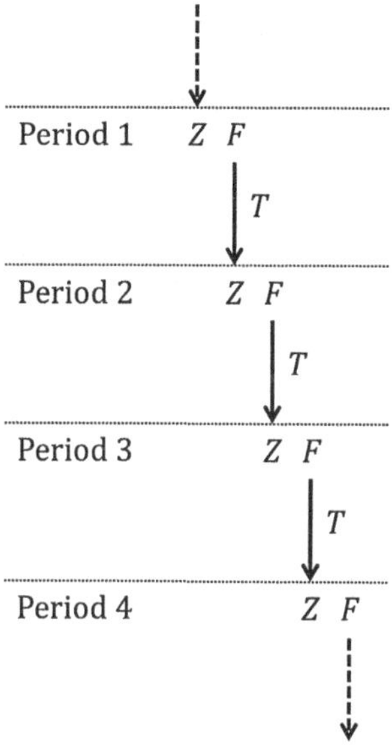

Fig. 2.5 A recurring process that uses factor *F* to produce consumer good *Z* and that lasts for a duration *T*

need can still be met but not the future one (assuming *Z* is non-durable). Due to time preference, immediate needs hold more value than future ones, so in period 2 (and in any other period), the consumer good *Z* has a higher value than its factor *F*.

This difference in valuation, caused by the duration of the production process, results in a ***discounted*** value of the factor relative to its product. Mises (1998 [1949]) refers to this valuation difference as "originary interest." This gap arises here entirely from the preference for the present. Additionally, it is evident that the longer the duration *T* of the process, the larger the discount applied, resulting in a lower relative value of the factor compared to the product, all else being equal.

2.3.6 Opportunity Cost

Böhm-Bawerk (1959a [1884], p. 185) provides an example of an individual who uses a group of factors *G* to produce good *Z*. What is the "cost" of obtaining good *Z*? In other words, what sacrifice did the individual have to make to produce *Z*? The "direct" cost is apparent, as Böhm-Bawerk points out, because to acquire good *Z*, the individual must sacrifice

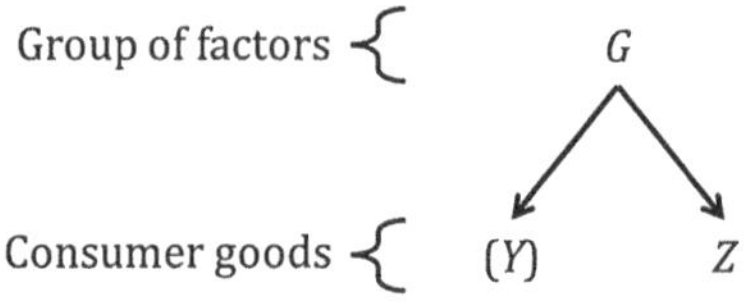

Fig. 2.6 The cost of producing *Z* is the value of the next valued good *Υ* that can be produced with *Z*

the factors *G*. However, what does this sacrifice signify from a subjective perspective? To understand this, we need to determine the satisfaction or value the individual relinquished to obtain *Z*. If *Z* had not been produced, the factors *G* would have been used to create another good, let us say *Υ* (which assumes these factors are convertible), as illustrated in Fig. 2.6.

This "indirect" cost, which Böhm-Bawerk refers to, is subjective and has later been called "opportunity cost." If the factors *G* are purely specific and can produce nothing other than *Z*, then their opportunity cost is zero, as they have no alternative use. Only convertible goods are "costly," as their application in one process rather than another requires a choice, thus necessitating a sacrifice. According to Mises (1998 [1949], p. 206), every action aims to achieve a psychic profit, defined as the positive difference between the value of the objective pursued and its opportunity cost, that is, between the value of the produced good (*Z*) and that of the alternative use of the means employed to produce it (*Υ*).

Thirlby (1981 [1946], pp. 138–141) summarizes this theory of subjective opportunity cost by stating that when an actor faces a choice between two actions, selecting one over the other incurs a cost equivalent to what they would have gained by choosing the alternative action. This cost is not measured in goods, particularly not in terms of money spent one way or another. It is subjective, known only to the actors themselves, and contingent upon the options they are aware of. As the actors are not omniscient, many potential alternatives remain unknown, thus not influencing their choices. A change in circumstances or the discovery of new options may compel them to reevaluate their decisions, incurring new costs. The cost is "ephemeral" in that once the action is executed, it ceases to hold any significance for the actor, who will then encounter new alternatives and, consequently, new costs. As long as a production decision proceeds as planned, it does not necessitate a choice, and the actor incurs no subjective cost, even if various resources must be expended in the process.

References

Čuhel, F. (1907). *Zur Lehre von den Bedürfnissen*. Wagner.

Fetter, F. (1915). *Economic Principles*. Century.

Hülsmann, J. G. (2007). *Mises. The Last Knight of Liberalism*. Ludwig von Mises Institute.

Hülsmann, J. G. (2024). *Abundance, Generosity, and the State. An Inquiry into Economic Principles*. Ludwig von Mises Institute.

Menger, C. (1976 [1871]). *Principles of Economics*. New York University Press.

Pareto, V. (1981 [1909]). *Manuel d'Économie Politique*. Droz.

Robbins, L. (1932). *An Essay on the Nature and Significance of Economic Science*. Macmillan.

Rothbard, M. N. (1956). Toward a Reconstruction of Utility and Welfare Economics. In M. Sennholz (Ed.), *On Freedom and Free Enterprise. Essays in Honor of Ludwig von Mises* (pp. 224–262). Princeton.

Rothbard, M. N. (1962). *Man, Economy, and State. A Treatise on Economic Principles*. D. Van Nostrand.

Samuelson, P. A. (1954). The Pure Theory of Public Expenditure. *Review of Economics and Statistics, 36*(4), 387–389.

Smith, A. (1976 [1776]). *An Inquiry into the Nature and Causes of the Wealth of Nations*. The University of Chicago Press.

Thirlby, G. F. (1981 [1946]). The Subjective Theory of Value and Accounting "Cost". In J. Buchanan & G. F. Thirlby (Eds.), *L.S.E. Essays on Cost* (pp. 137–161). New York University Press.

von Böhm-Bawerk, E. (1959a [1884]). *History and Critique of Interest Theories*. Libertarian Press.

von Böhm-Bawerk, E. (1959b [1889]). *Positive Theory of Capital*. Libertarian Press.

von Böhm-Bawerk, E. (1962 [1881]). Whether Legal Rights and Relationships Are Economic Goods. In E. von Böhm-Bawerk (Ed.), *Shorter Classics of Böhm-Bawerk* (Vol. 1, pp. 25–138). Libertarian Press.

von Mises, L. (1980 [1912]). *The Theory of Money and Credit*. LibertyClassics.

von Mises, L. (1998 [1949]). *Human Action. A Treatise on Economics*. Ludwig von Mises Institute.

von Wieser, F. (1884). *Über den Ursprung und die Hauptgesetze des Wirthschaftlichen Werthes*. Alfred Hölder.

von Wieser, F. (1893 [1889]). *Natural Value*. Macmillan.

CHAPTER 3

Exchange and Price

Abstract Menger explains exchange as a means of satisfying needs more effectively through trade, where each party subjectively values what they receive more than what they give up. Historically, exchange evolved from barter to monetary systems, facilitating the division of labor and increasing productive efficiency. Prices, as exchange ratios, arise in each market from the subjective valuations of buyers and sellers, and they are governed by the law of supply and demand. They also play a coordinating role between markets by enabling entrepreneurial activity to adapt the economic system to dynamic changes in consumer demand, technology, and resource availability—as explained by the principle of profit rate equalization.

Keywords Exchange • Market prices • Dynamic changes

Menger's third major contribution, an application of his value theory, is a theory of exchange. It explains why individuals trade goods based on the principle of double inequality of values and how exchange rates—that is, prices—are determined. His successors, most notably Böhm-Bawerk (1959 [1889]), further developed a theory of the price system that reinterpreted the classical economists' "law of costs" within the framework of the imputation principle, where costs are explained by prices rather than

R. Fillieule, *The Austrian School of Economics*, Palgrave Studies in Austrian Economics,
https://doi.org/10.1007/978-3-031-83414-1_3

the other way around. Contributions from the American School, particularly Clark's (1899) work on dynamic change and Knight's (1921) insights on profit, were later incorporated by Mises (1998 [1949]) into the Austrian theory of the price system. This theory is fundamentally different from both partial and general equilibrium theory and goes beyond the traditional division between microeconomics and macroeconomics.

3.1 The Theory of Exchange

3.1.1 Forms of Social Interaction

In his treatise, Menger focuses solely on one form of goods circulation between individuals: exchange. In contrast, Mises (1998 [1949]) develops a broader framework that distinguishes between two types of human interaction: "autistic action" and cooperative relations. Cooperative relations are further divided into two categories—contractual and hegemonic:

1. *"Autistic" action*: This involves no expectation of reciprocity and can occur either in isolation or without expecting anything in return from others (e.g., the act of giving).
2. *Contractual relations*: These involve exchange, where one party voluntarily gives up a good to another to receive a good voluntarily given up by the other party.
3. *Hegemonic relations*: These are asymmetrical relationships in which one party or group, under duress (due to fear of violent consequences), obeys the commands of another party or group without any pre-agreed exchange. Examples Mises provides include relationships between masters and slaves, lords and serfs, parents and children, or the State and its citizens.

3.1.2 Explaining Exchange

Menger begins by examining the simplest form of exchange, where mutual benefits are most obvious: one actor has an excess of good *A* but lacks good *B*, while another actor has an excess of good *B* but lacks good *A*. If the first actor gives up their surplus of good *A* and the second gives up their surplus of good *B*, both improve the satisfaction of their needs without any real sacrifice (except for costs directly related to the exchange itself, which will be discussed later).

In most cases, however, exchange involves some sacrifice, as each actor could have used the goods given up to meet some of their own needs. Yet, they choose to exchange because the good they receive allows them to satisfy needs they consider more important than those they are foregoing. In other words, for both participants, the good they receive has a higher subjective value than the one they give up. Menger (1976 [1871]) identifies three conditions that must be met for two actors to engage in an exchange:

1. *Awareness*: Both actors know what the other is willing to trade.
2. *Ability*: There are no physical or legal obstacles preventing the transfer of goods.
3. *Value*: Each actor values the good received more than the good given up (a principle Rothbard calls "double inequality of values").

If any one of these conditions is not met, the exchange—defined as a voluntary transfer of goods—does not take place. Condition (3) highlights that the reason for exchanging is the actors' desire for a greater satisfaction of their needs. It also shows that exchanges do not involve equality of value: people do not trade goods of equal subjective value, but rather goods with differing values. If the values were equal, there would be no motivation to exchange (see Hülsmann, 2024, Chap. 7, for an in-depth critique of the mistaken idea that there is "equivalence" in exchange).

3.1.3 Exchange at a Fixed Price

Menger explores the limits of exchange in the simple case where the price between two goods is fixed. Imagine one person owns a stock of good *A* and another owns a stock of good *B*, and they agree to trade at a fixed rate of one-for-one. As they start exchanging, the first person's stock of *A* decreases while their stock of *B* increases, and the reverse happens for the second person. According to the law of marginal utility: for the first person, the marginal utility of *A* increases and that of *B* decreases; for the second person, the marginal utility of *A* decreases and that of *B* increases. The exchange continues as long as, for each person, the marginal utility of the good given up is lower than that of the good received. If both have large enough stocks, a point will be reached where, for one of them, the marginal utility of the good being given up eventually surpasses the utility of the good received. At that point, the exchange no longer adds value, so the person decides to stop. The exchange reaches its limit and stops, even if the other party is still willing to continue trading.

3.1.4 Exchange and Value Maximization

The previous scenario can be generalized to involve multiple goods, helping us understand how an individual maximizes satisfaction from their resources. Suppose a person has a stock of good *A* (resources) that can be exchanged against other goods *B*, *C*, and *D*. The exchange rates between these goods are fixed at 1:1, such as $1A \leftrightarrow 1B$, $1A \leftrightarrow 1C$, and $1A \leftrightarrow 1D$. To maximize satisfaction, the individual will make successive exchanges, starting with the one that offers the most satisfaction for each unit of *A*. After each exchange, the individual reassesses the new marginal utilities and continues exchanging for the next good that provides the greatest satisfaction.

As more exchanges occur, the marginal utility of *A* increases, while the marginal utilities of *B*, *C*, and *D* decrease, according to the law of marginal utility. Eventually, the individual reaches a point where further exchanges no longer offer an advantage, and the marginal utilities of *A*, *B*, *C*, and *D*, are as close as possible. If goods were infinitely divisible, this process would result in the equality of marginal utilities, but because goods are not perfectly divisible, differences between marginal utilities persist (Böhm-Bawerk, 1959 [1889], p. 173).

Neoclassical economists have developed advanced mathematical models to formalize this kind of optimization of subjective value (a topic referred to as "consumer theory" in textbooks). However, it is important to note that these examples of fixed-price exchanges are somewhat artificial, as they assume that subjective preferences adjust to pre-existing prices when from a broader theoretical perspective, prices are determined by the subjective preferences and choices of individuals (see Sect. 3.2.15).

3.1.5 Productivity and Costs of Exchange

Exchange is productive because it creates wealth in a similar way to increasing the number of physical goods, as it allows individuals to better satisfy their needs. Professions that facilitate exchanges, such as intermediaries, are therefore just as productive as those in agriculture or industry. Menger's understanding of exchange productivity is rooted in a subjective value framework. An objective analysis, by contrast, would mistakenly conclude that exchange creates no wealth, as the goods being traded already existed, implying that all the wealth was "already there." However, since preferences are subjective, known only to the individuals involved and changing over time, only a subjectivist analysis can accurately assess the productivity of exchange.

Menger also points out that exchange always involves costs, known today as "transaction costs" (Coase, 1937). These include time spent on the transaction, insurance, and commissions, as well as costs that resemble production expenses, such as transportation, packaging, storage, customs duties, and other trade taxes. An exchange will only occur if the benefits for each participant outweigh these costs.

3.1.6 Use Value and Exchange Value

For an isolated individual, goods can satisfy needs only through their direct use. However, when exchange becomes possible, an individual faces two choices: to use the good themselves or to trade it for another good. When the good possessed is used directly, it provides what Menger calls its "use value." When exchange is possible, it also takes on an "exchange value," defined by the use value of the good received in return. This exchange value reflects the best possible trade opportunity available to the individual, representing the highest value they believe they can obtain through exchanging.

Some goods have use value but no exchange value, like a family photo. On the other hand, in a developed economy, many goods have exchange value but no use value, such as an optician's stock of prescription glasses. Some goods have both use and exchange value, and in these cases, the value of the good is the greater of the two. The individual will choose to exchange if the exchange value of their good exceeds its use value, meaning the needs met with the good obtained in the trade are more important than those met by using the original good. If the use value is higher, the individual will keep the good for personal use.

At any given time, changes in preferences or available stocks can shift what Menger calls a good's "center of gravity," meaning that its exchange value may rise above or fall below its use value.

3.1.7 Exchange and Division of Labor

When two individuals produce consumer goods, *A* and *B*, the possibility of exchanging part of their output encourages them to specialize in producing one good each, thereby increasing overall consumption. This efficiency of the division of labor is most obvious when one person is better at producing *A* and the other is better at producing *B* (law of absolute advantage). As Ricardo (1951 [1817]) demonstrated in his theory of international trade, the division of labor is beneficial even when one individual is more efficient at producing both goods. In this case, the more efficient person should specialize in the activity where their superiority is greatest, known as the law of comparative advantage, later renamed the *law of association* by Mises. The possibility of exchange facilitates the division of labor, which in turn boosts production and fosters further exchange (Rothbard, 1962, pp. 80–81). Specialization will become more extensive when individuals expect to trade a larger portion of their output, echoing Adam Smith's famous observation that "the division of labor is limited by the extent of the market."

3.1.8 Commodities and "Marketability"

In the most basic economic system, individuals produce goods solely for personal consumption. As the system becomes more complex due to exchange and the division of labor, people begin producing goods to trade them for goods made by others. However, they will only produce for others when they are reasonably certain they will be able to exchange these goods at the end of the production process. In a more developed exchange system, individuals produce *commodities*—goods they keep ready for potential buyers. In this case, producers do not wait for a confirmed customer but complete the production and store the goods, expecting future buyers (Menger, 1976 [1871], p. 238).

The concept of a commodity, like value and goods, must be understood within a subjectivist framework: it is not an inherent characteristic of goods but a relationship between individuals and goods. For example, if a hatmaker decides to keep one of the hats for personal use, it immediately loses its status as a commodity and becomes a consumer good. More broadly, once a good reaches its final user, it ceases to be a commodity and becomes a consumer good.

The *marketability* of a commodity refers to its ability to be sold, that is, exchanged for other goods. Its marketability depends on several factors: the number of potential buyers, how easily it can be transported, its value, the geographical area and time period over which it can be sold, and the efficiency of the markets where it is traded. For instance, a stock of wheat is far more "marketable" than a stock of fur, as it appeals to a larger number of people, across broader regions and timeframes, and is traded on more organized markets.

3.1.9 From Barter to Monetary Exchange

Initially, exchange takes the form of barter, where individuals trade goods they intend to use themselves, either for consumption or to produce other goods. However, as Menger points out, this form of exchange faces significant limitations. Each individual must find a trading partner who not only has the exact good they need but also desires the good they are offering. This double coincidence of wants is often difficult to achieve, especially for goods with low marketability, like large or indivisible items. For example, the owner of a horse seeking to trade it for food and clothes will struggle to find someone who possesses those specific items and wishes to exchange them for a horse. Barter, or direct exchange, thus faces considerable practical obstacles.

One way to overcome these difficulties is through *indirect exchange*. If the horse owner cannot find a direct trade partner, they might sell the horse for more exchangeable goods, even if those goods are not immediately useful to them. These more widely demanded goods will be easier to trade later for the food and clothes they originally sought. In doing so, the owner avoids the deadlock of direct barter and moves closer to their goal.

Since it benefits every participant to exchange their goods for more "marketable" items, indirect exchange becomes widespread. This practice not only deepens the division of labor but also increases demand for the most exchangeable goods in the economy. These goods are now sought not just for direct use, but also for their usefulness in further exchanges. As demand for these goods grows, their value and marketability increase further. This process, driven by circular causality, eventually leads to a small number of goods becoming systematically used in indirect exchanges. These goods, when accepted by all economic actors because they can be easily traded for what they want, become *money*.

Menger demonstrates how direct barter transitions into indirect and then monetary exchange, elevating the division of labor—and consequently, productivity—to levels that would be impossible without money.

3.2 The System of Market Prices

3.2.1 *The Concept of Price*

A price represents the rate at which goods are exchanged. For example, if two people trade 3 apples for 2 pears, the price of one apple (in terms of pears) is 2/3 of a pear, and the price of one pear (in terms of apples) is 3/2 apples. In a monetary economy, prices are typically expressed in money, but we could also express the price of money in goods. For instance, if a television costs $449, the price of one dollar in terms of that television is 1/449.

For Menger, the concept of price originates from exchange, which itself arises from the basic economic drive of individuals to better satisfy their needs. He emphasizes that price does not indicate an equality of value between goods. Nineteenth-century Classical economists tried to explain prices by claiming goods had equal value: for example, a table costing five times as much as a chair was said to "equal" five chairs in value. They attempted to justify this equality through the labor theory of value or the equal costs of production. Menger criticized this as a serious error that caused "incalculable damage" to economics. In reality, price is the result of exchange, which in turn reflects *inequality* in subjective values, not equality.

3.2.2 *The Auction Market (Law of Supply and Demand)*

Menger (1976 [1871]), Böhm-Bawerk (1959 [1889], p. 220), and later Rothbard (1962, p. 206) use the auction market model to explain price theory. This model, familiar from introductory economics textbooks, shows how prices are formed through market interactions between buyers and sellers.

Demand is the relationship between various possible prices of a good and the quantity buyers are willing to purchase at each price, assuming all other factors remain constant. This is shaped by buyers' subjective preferences between money and the good. According to the law of marginal utility, demand decreases as price increases (*law of demand*), meaning higher prices lead to lower quantities demanded, all else being equal.

Supply, on the other hand, is the relationship between different prices of a good and the quantity sellers are willing to offer at each price, again assuming other factors remain constant. Unlike demand, the supply curve's slope can vary. While supply often increases with price, there are cases where it may decrease. A classic example is labor: if wages rise high enough, a worker might choose to reduce hours worked to enjoy more leisure, hence a decreasing supply of labor as a function of its price.

Let us take the typical case of increasing supply (see Fig. 3.1). If the market price is above the ***equilibrium price*** where demand and supply meet, the quantity supplied will exceed the quantity demanded, leading to competition among sellers, who have to lower the price to be able to sell. Conversely, if the price is below equilibrium, buyers will compete, and sellers will be able to raise the price. In both scenarios, the market price moves toward equilibrium. This auction model allows us to understand, within a consistent and comprehensive framework, the traditional ***law of supply and demand***: if supply increases (shifting the supply curve to the right), the equilibrium price tends to fall; if demand increases (shifting the demand curve to the right), the equilibrium price tends to rise.

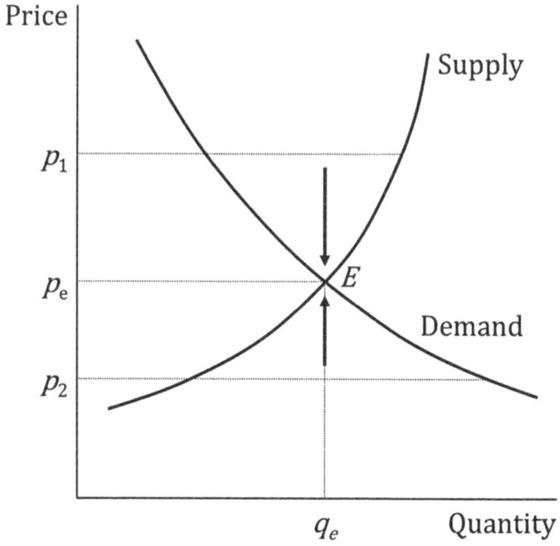

Fig. 3.1 Determination of the auction price (law of supply and demand)

3.2.3 *The Classical Version of the Law of Costs*

Böhm-Bawerk (1959 [1889], pp. 248–256) provides detailed insights into the relationship between prices and monetary costs. He supports the law of costs, which states that the price of a good that can be reproduced indefinitely will not remain above or below its production cost for long. He finds the arguments of Adam Smith (1976 [1776], Chap. 7) and Ricardo (1951 [1817], Chap. 4) perfectly valid. He summarizes them as follows: if the price of a good rises significantly above production costs, producers enjoy windfall profits, which incentivize them to increase production and attract new competitors into the market. As a result, supply rises, pushing price down and eventually eliminating those windfall profits. On the other hand, if the price drops below production costs, producers suffer losses, prompting them to reduce production or exit the market entirely. As supply decreases, price rises, and losses disappear.

However, Böhm-Bawerk (1962 [1894]) notes that classical economists, including Alfred Marshall (1920 [1890]), were often unclear about the notion of cost. Sometimes, they interpreted cost as a monetary expense, while at other times, they referred to it as a sacrifice of labor ("real cost"). According to Böhm-Bawerk, the real-cost interpretation is incorrect. For example, a skilled worker does not sacrifice more than an unskilled worker, yet skilled labor costs more in monetary terms. It is this monetary cost, rather than the labor sacrifice, that must be considered under the law of costs.

3.2.4 *Reversing Classical Causality: Costs Determined by Prices*

Böhm-Bawerk shows that the law of monetary costs must be reinterpreted in light of Menger's principle of imputation. Contrary to what Classical economists believed, costs do not determine prices; rather, prices determine costs.

He takes the example of products that use iron as a production factor, simplifying by ignoring other factors like labor and the interest rate. Consumers create demand for iron-based products, and sellers supply them, establishing the (equilibrium) prices of those products. Producers, in turn, use these prices to determine how much they are willing to pay for iron. If the price of a product is high enough, say $10, producers are willing to pay up to $10 per unit of iron, which they need to produce the equilibrium quantity of their product (assuming each unit of the product requires one unit of iron). If the product price is $9, producers will not pay more than $9 per unit of iron, and so on down the line. The final price of iron is determined by the balance between demand for iron and its supply, which might settle at, say, $3 per unit. All producers whose products sell for $3 or more can then afford to buy iron and produce their goods.

Böhm-Bawerk points out that the price of iron ($3) is the result of a causal chain that starts with consumers' subjective evaluations of iron products. These subjective evaluations lead to the prices of iron-based products, which then determine the cost of iron itself. This reasoning exemplifies the law of marginal utility, where the price of iron is determined by its "marginal" use, meaning the lowest monetary value attributed to it by consumers who are able to buy iron products ($3 in this case).

This line of reasoning also highlights the *causal* nature of Austrian economics (Rothbard, 1962, p. 277). In Austrian theory, values and prices are not mutually determined in a general equilibrium; instead, they follow an order of causality that starts with the subjective needs of individuals. From there, the chain of causality moves to goods that satisfy those needs directly (first-order goods), then to goods used to produce first-order goods (second-order goods), and so on, extending all the way back to the original factors of production.

3.2.5 *Convergence to Equilibrium Through Disappearance of Entrepreneurial Profits and Losses*

Böhm-Bawerk's analysis goes further. In a market where iron products sell at prices ranging from $10 to $1, even though each product contains only one unit of iron priced at $3, some producers will earn entrepreneurial profits (e.g., those selling at $8 for a product that costs them only $3) while others incur entrepreneurial losses (e.g., those selling at $1 or $2). As a result, capitalist investors will:

1. reduce investment in unprofitable sectors, decreasing supply and driving up prices in those markets;
2. increase investment in profitable sectors, raising supply and pushing prices down.

This process of capital reallocation continues as long as profitability differences persist across industries. Ultimately, product prices will converge to $3, aligning with production costs and observing the law of costs (price

= costs). At this equilibrium, all consumers willing to pay at least $3 for iron products will be able to purchase them. Böhm-Bawerk notes that this adjustment process can also affect the price of iron. For instance, if consumers willing to pay $4 for iron products deplete all available stocks, the price of iron will rise from $3 to $4, further reinforcing the idea that it is not costs that determine prices, but rather the other way around.

3.2.6 *An Apparent Case of Cost-Based Pricing*

Now consider a scenario where the supply of iron increases, either due to the discovery of richer mines or due to the implementation of a more efficient production process. As the price of iron falls, the price of iron products will also decrease. Does this suggest that lower production costs (of iron) influence product prices? Böhm-Bawerk's response is negative. He demonstrates—by tracing back to the original factor of labor—that even in this case, the causal chain runs from product prices to production costs.

Suppose a day's work is paid $1, a wage determined by imputation from the prices of labor's final products (since labor is an original, non-produced factor, it doesn't have a production cost, and the law of costs cannot be applied to it). If it previously took 3 days of work to produce one unit of iron, but now only 2 days are needed, the cost of producing iron is now $2, though its price remains $3. This assumes no change in production output, meaning labor input has decreased, keeping production levels steady. The profitability of this sector will attract additional capital, leading to the hiring of more workers and increased iron production until the exceptional profits disappear—this happens when the price of iron falls to $2 (2 days of labor at $1/day). As iron production increases, the price of iron products also falls, from $3 to $2.

Thus, the price of consumer goods determines the price of labor, which in turn determines the price of iron. The price of iron, then, is dictated by the prices of consumer goods as reflected in labor costs. Even in this case, the fundamental determination of costs arises from the prices of final goods, reaffirming a key principle from subjective value theory (see Sect. 2.3.4).

3.2.7 *The Marginal Nominal Product*

The reasoning outlined above relies on two significant simplifying assumptions. The first is that iron is the sole factor of production. Böhm-Bawerk acknowledges this limitation, noting that any good is produced through the combination of multiple factors, each contributing only a fraction of the overall selling price. Rothbard (1962) proposed a broader analysis of factor pricing that incorporates this complexity through the concept of the "marginal value product."

A producer assesses the value of a unit of a factor (keeping the stocks of other factors constant) based on its marginal nominal product, which represents the income that would be forfeited if that unit was lost. Understanding his production function, the producer knows that with this unit, a quantity q_2 will be produced, while without it, only a lesser quantity q_1 will be produced: $q_1 < q_2$. Given the demand for the product, if q_2 is produced, the price will be p_2, and if q_1 is produced will be $p_1 > p_2$, since supply would be reduced. Therefore, the marginal nominal product of this unit is given by $p_2q_2 - p_1q_1$, which reflects the maximum amount the producer is willing to pay for that unit. Rothbard mathematically demonstrates that production can only occur in a range where the marginal nominal product decreases as the quantity produced increases. Since the marginal nominal product also reflects the demand for the factor, this demand diminishes for each individual producer. Consequently, market demand—the aggregate of all individual demands—also decreases. The interaction of this demand with the supply of the factor determines its price (the equilibrium market price of the factor). This price serves as a monetary opportunity cost, indicating what each producer is willing to pay for an additional unit of the good.

3.2.8 *Discounting*

Böhm-Bawerk's reasoning is also based on a second simplification, which involves disregarding the passage of time and, consequently, the rate of interest. However, he is aware that producers consider the duration of the process in which a factor is utilized by discounting the future price of their product at the interest rate. For example, assume the annual interest rate is 5%. If the time between purchasing the unit of the factor and selling the product is 1 year, and the producer estimates that this "last" unit of the factor will yield \$105 after 1 year, he would be willing to pay up to \$100 today for that unit (because \$100 multiplied by (1 + 5%) equals \$105). If the price exceeds \$100—say, \$101—the return from using that unit would only yield an interest of 3.96% = (105 – 101)/101, which is less favorable than the current interest rate of 5%. Thus, the producer would have no incentive to invest \$101 more in this process, as a better return could be earned elsewhere. Rothbard addresses both of Böhm-Bawerk's simplifying assumptions by introducing the concept of "discounted marginal value product," leading to the general principle that *factor prices are determined by the imputation of discounted marginal value products.*

3.2.9 From "Frictional Obstacles" to "Dynamic Changes"

In the real historical world, the law of costs is never strictly adhered to. In some industries or companies, prices may exceed costs, while in others, prices may fall below costs for varying periods. These discrepancies arise from what Böhm-Bawerk refers to as "frictional obstacles." Technical progress and unforeseen changes in supply and demand continually create positive or negative deviations between prices and costs. These gaps serve as sources of profit and loss that entrepreneurial activity addresses by reallocating capital among different branches and stages of production. However, the term "frictional obstacle" is somewhat misleading, as it conflates the forces that drive prices away from costs with those that merely slow down the adjustment process between prices and costs.

The second generation of Austrian economists, including Mises and Schumpeter, drew inspiration from the analysis of these phenomena proposed by American economist John Bates Clark (1899, p. 56). Clark established the Neoclassical theory of the dynamics of capitalism by distinguishing between different types of *dynamic changes* that alter the productive system. In his own words, these changes alter "the relative sizes of the different industrial groups." He identifies five key types: (1) population growth, (2) an increase in capital, (3) improvements in production methods, (4) the selection of the most efficient industrial plants (resulting in the disappearance of the least efficient), and (5) the multiplication of consumer needs. Mises (1981 [1922]) proposes a six-category typology explicitly inspired by Clark's framework, which includes natural changes, changes in the quantity and quality of the population, changes in the quantity and quality of capital goods, changes in production techniques, changes in the organization of labor, and changes in demand. Schumpeter (2021 [1911]) popularized a slightly different classification that emphasizes what he terms "new combinations"—qualitative innovations that transform the production structure, such as new goods, new production methods, new distribution channels, new sources of raw materials, and new organizational forms (e.g., the emergence of trusts or monopolies).

3.2.10 Monetary Profits and Losses

Entrepreneurial monetary profit refers to the positive difference between the selling price and the comprehensive monetary production cost, which includes the average interest rate. (Strictly speaking, interest is not a cost but rather an income of production; see Sect. 6.2.1.) If the income from sales fails to cover these broad costs, the entrepreneur incurs a loss.

The Austrian School was significantly influenced by Knight (1921) regarding the origin of profits and losses. He argues that dynamic changes alone cannot fully explain entrepreneurial profits and losses within an economic system. If entrepreneurs correctly anticipate a change, they will make timely adjustments that eliminate potential sources of profit or loss. For instance, if entrepreneurs foresee a sharp increase in the price of wheat a month from now, they will reserve quantities of wheat for resale, which will ultimately lower the future price. While current wheat owners might profit from the rising prices, this profit arises from the fact that the anticipated future price increase was not accurately predicted beforehand. Had it been anticipated, the opportunity for future profit would have already vanished.

Knight concludes that profits and losses arise from a discrepancy between the current situation and what was expected by economic agents. This misjudgment stems from the inherent *uncertainty* of the future. It is essential to differentiate this uncertainty, which leads to profits and losses, from "risk," which can be quantified by tracking the frequency of certain events. Uncertainty, in this context, cannot be measured through frequency calculations, as it pertains to a unique set of causal factors, some of which remain unknown. Mises (1998 [1949], p. 291) supports Knight's perspective, asserting that uncertainty surrounding future supply and demand is the "ultimate source" of entrepreneurial profit and loss.

3.2.11 The Tendency Toward Equal Rates of Return

When monetary profits and losses arise in the economic system due to errors in anticipation, entrepreneurial actions will tend to eliminate these discrepancies, thereby equalizing rates of return. These rates are defined as the relative difference between the selling price p of one unit of product and the production cost per unit c: $(p - c)/c$. When a firm, branch, or production stage experiences entrepreneurial profit, it attracts investment, leading to two main consequences:

1. The increased production of the good boosts supply, which *lowers the selling price.*
2. These additional investments raise the demand for necessary factors of production, which tends to increase the prices of these factors, thereby *raising unitary production costs.*

As a result of this dual effect—falling prices and rising costs—profits tend to diminish, and the rate of return for the firm, branch, or production stage reverts to the average. Conversely, when entrepreneurial losses occur, a symmetrical process takes place: prices rise while costs fall, eliminating these losses and bringing the rate of return back to the average for the economic system. Consequently, there is a persistent tendency for rates of return in a market economy to equalize (Reisman, 1996, pp. 172–187).

It is important to note that, since individuals aim to maximize their subjective satisfaction rather than merely their monetary income, rates of return may differ across industries, even in a state of final equilibrium. For example, if individuals are morally hesitant to invest in certain sectors (such as arms or tobacco), the equilibrium rate of return in those industries will be higher. Conversely, industries that provide greater satisfaction to investors through their financing will experience lower equilibrium rates of return (Rothbard, 1962, p. 378).

3.2.12 The Evenly Rotating Economy

Hypothetically, if no further dynamic changes were to occur in the economy—meaning there are no shifts in individual preferences, production techniques, or resource availability—the system would eventually converge toward a state of static equilibrium, which Mises (1998 [1949]) refers to as the "evenly rotating economy" (ERE). In this uniform rotation scenario, an imaginary construct that cannot exist in reality, there would be no entrepreneurial profit or loss, as the same activities would be performed in the same manner, period after period.

In this context, the prices of produced goods represent the "natural" prices of the Classical economists, the "static" prices as defined by Clark (1899), and the "final" prices identified by Mises. All of these prices equal the costs of factor production plus interest on invested capital. The concept of the uniform rotation economy serves as a theoretical framework for analyzing the long-term effects of dynamic change. It also underscores the contrast with real-world market conditions, where constant imbalances cause both minor and significant discrepancies between prices and average costs across different firms and industries.

3.2.13 *Adaptation Processes to the Main Types of Dynamic Change*

The three primary types of dynamic market shocks are demand shocks, technical shocks, and resource shocks. The adaptation processes to these shocks illustrate the principle of the trend toward equal rates of return.

Resource Shock: In his most famous paper, Hayek (1945) examines the implications of tin scarcity. Assuming a reduced supply of this raw material (whatever the cause), its owners can command higher prices. Companies that rely on tin will tend to switch to nearby substitutes, thus increasing the demand for these alternatives and driving up their prices. This, in turn, raises the costs for firms using tin or its substitutes (all else being equal), leading to a reduction in their rates of return. Consequently, capital—and hence factors of production—tends to be reallocated to sectors that utilize less tin or its substitutes. Firms that employ these scarcer resources will save on costs by contracting their operations, which helps restore their rate of return.

Technical Progress: Hazlitt (1946) presents a scenario in which a company in a specific industry (A) adopts a new type of machine to reduce production costs. Initially, this firm enjoys higher profits, attracting capital and encouraging other companies in industry A to adopt the same methods. As competition increases and more capital flows into the industry, production rises, and the reduced costs eventually lead to a lower selling price for good A:

1. If the demand facing industry A is *elastic*, the increase in production (q_A) leads to a rise in total revenue ($p_A \times q_A$), since the higher output (q_A) more than compensates for the lower price (p_A). As a result, industry A experiences an above-average rate of return, attracting even more capital until its returns normalize to the average. This growth comes at the expense of industries producing substitutes, which face declining demand, falling prices, losses, and eventual contraction.
2. On the other hand, if the demand is *inelastic*, total revenue ($p_A \times q_A$) in industry A decreases, as the lower price (p_A) outweighs the higher

output (q_A). Consequently, industry A suffers from a below-average rate of return, causing capital and resources to shift back into other industries where they can be used more productively. This scenario is especially beneficial, as it not only increases the production of good A but also boosts the production of other goods.

Change in Demand: Reisman (1996) analyzes the effects of shifts in consumer preferences. If consumers decide to purchase more of good A and less of good B, the price of A will tend to rise due to increased demand, resulting in profits and capital inflows. Conversely, the price of B will decrease, leading to losses for its producers and an outflow of capital. Consequently, industry A expands while industry B contracts and their respective rates of profitability return to the mean. If factors of production can be easily converted from one industry to another, these effects will largely remain confined to the two initially impacted sectors. However, if conversion is difficult or impossible, the repercussions may extend upstream: the price of factors used to produce A will tend to rise, leading to expansion in upstream industries, while the price of factors used to produce B will decline, causing upstream branches to contract.

These price theory models transcend the conventional distinction between microeconomics and macroeconomics, as they assess the impact of dynamic changes on the overall organization of the economic system, considering both horizontal and vertical interactions between markets.

3.2.14 *The Rationality of the Market Economy*

Austrian price theory illustrates how the system of market exchange coordinates all economic activities by optimizing the use of production factors. When demand for a good increases (or decreases), the market economy responds by expanding (or contracting) the production branch associated with that good, as well as its upstream industries. In cases of technical progress within a sector, if demand is elastic, the market promotes growth in that sector and its upstream industries, while negatively impacting branches producing substitutes. Conversely, if demand is inelastic, the sector and its associated industries will contract, benefiting substitute industries and increasing overall production within the system. Finally, when an original factor of production becomes scarce, producers are compelled to conserve it, seek substitutes, and reduce their activities in favor of those that do not rely on the scarcer factor. Thus, the market economy demonstrates its ability to adapt to various types of shocks by allocating productive resources *as if the decisions were made by a single rational actor* (Hayek, 1945).

3.2.15 Entrepreneurs and Consumer Sovereignty

Market data is in a constant state of flux, requiring the production structure to adapt. However, this adaptation is not automatic; *it is driven by consumer preferences, guided by entrepreneurs, and executed by owners of production factors* (workers, landowners, and capitalists).

This dynamic is particularly evident when there is a shift in consumer demand. The sooner entrepreneurs can anticipate these changes, the more profits they can generate by reallocating production factors to sectors that consumers now value, thereby avoiding losses in areas that have become less desirable. Entrepreneurs who fail to recognize these shifts or who resist consumer preferences risk incurring significant losses and may lose their entrepreneurial status by depleting their capital and losing the confidence of potential investors.

A similar principle applies in the context of technological advancements. When a profitable new technique emerges that can lower costs and selling prices, entrepreneurs who adopt this innovation quickly stand to benefit significantly, while those who hesitate or refuse to adapt will suffer the consequences. This occurs because consumers tend to seek the best value for their money and will shift their spending toward businesses offering more favorable terms—essentially rewarding innovative companies while penalizing those that lag behind.

In this sense, consumers act as the "sovereigns" of the market process, as they ultimately validate or undermine entrepreneurs' plans. Their spending choices indirectly dictate how capital is allocated across different production branches and compel profit-seeking entrepreneurs to minimize production costs. Moreover, consumers influence the overall level of capital accumulation through their choices regarding intertemporal consumption and savings (see Sect. 5.1.11). When entrepreneurs misjudge consumer preferences or choose to defy them, they face losses that increase with the magnitude of their mistakes or the degree of their resistance.

The market process shares similarities with the political process of democratic elections, in which the majority vote brings politicians to power. However, significant differences exist between the political election process and the economic "election" of entrepreneurs through consumer purchases or abstentions. The economic "election" occurs continuously, not at several-year intervals, and can be reversed quickly. In a political election, the winning majority assumes complete control; in contrast, minority interests can sway economic outcomes. For instance, publishers cater to both mass audiences with popular genres and niche markets with complex philosophical or sophisticated artistic works.

Additionally, the impact of each economic "voter" depends on their consumption expenditure. A wealthier individual, who spends more, carries more weight in the economic "ballot" than someone with less financial means. Nonetheless, the overall consumption spending of the middle class collectively surpasses that of the wealthiest individuals, giving it a greater influence on the organization of production structures. Furthermore, income inequality arises from the market process itself, which is shaped by consumer choices that determine the prices of goods, which in turn affect the incomes of production factors, including wages for various types of skills (on these various points, see Mises, 1998 [1949], pp. 270–272).

Encroachments on consumer sovereignty primarily result from state intervention. When the government grants monopolistic privileges to certain producers, finances some public services through taxation, or imposes stringent regulations on companies, it effectively substitutes itself for consumers in deciding what should be produced, how, where, and in what quantities (see Chap. 9).

References

Clark, J. B. (1899). *The Distribution of Wealth. A Theory of Wages, Interest, and Profits.* Macmillan.

Coase, R. H. (1937). The Nature of the Firm. *Economica, 4*(16), 386–405.

Hayek, F. A. (1945). The Use of Knowledge in Society. *American Economic Review, 35*(4), 519–530.

Hazlitt, H. (1946). *Economics in One Lesson.* Harper & Brothers.

Hülsmann, J. G. (2024). *Abundance, Generosity, and the State. An Inquiry into Economic Principles.* Ludwig von Mises Institute.

Knight, F. H. (1921). *Risk, Uncertainty, and Profit.* Houghton Mifflin Company.

Marshall, A. (1920 [1890]). *Principles of Economics. An Introductory Volume.* Macmillan.

Menger, C. (1976 [1871]). *Principles of Economics.* New York University Press.

Reisman, G. (1996). *Capitalism. A Treatise on Economics.* Jameson Books.
Ricardo, D. (1951 [1817]). *On the Principles of Political Economy and Taxation.* Cambridge University Press.
Rothbard, M. N. (1962). *Man, Economy, and State. A Treatise on Economic Principles.* D. Van Nostrand.
Schumpeter, J. A. (2021 [1911]). *Theory of Economic Development.* Routledge.
Smith, A. (1976 [1776]). *An Inquiry into the Nature and Causes of the Wealth of Nations.* The University of Chicago Press.
von Böhm-Bawerk, E. (1959 [1889]). *Positive Theory of Capital.* Libertarian Press.
von Böhm-Bawerk, E. (1962 [1894]). The Ultimate Standard of Value. In E. von Böhm-Bawerk (Ed.), *Shorter Classics of Böhm-Bawerk* (Vol. 1, pp. 303–370). Libertarian Press.
von Mises, L. (1981 [1922]). *Socialism. An Economic and Sociological Analysis.* LibertyClassics.
von Mises, L. (1998 [1949]). *Human Action. A Treatise on Economics.* Ludwig von Mises Institute.

CHAPTER 4

Monopoly and Competition

Abstract The main monopoly theory developed by Austrian economists, from Menger to Mises, is the theory of monopoly price. However, this theory was later criticized within the Austrian School itself by Rothbard. On the topic of competition, Austrian economists critique standard models, such as perfect and monopolistic competition, for overlooking the dynamic and entrepreneurial nature of market processes. The chapter challenges the static assumptions of these models by highlighting instead entrepreneurial competition as a process of discovery, essential to the functioning of markets. Advertising, product differentiation, and cost-cutting are reframed as competitive, not monopolistic, elements.

Keywords Monopoly • Competition • Dynamics versus statics • Entrepreneurship

Monopoly theory has undergone significant development since Menger's initial formulation of the Austrian paradigm (1976 [1871]). Fetter (1915) and Mises (1998a [1944]) expanded on Menger's theory of monopoly pricing, but it was later criticized and rejected by Rothbard (1962). Starting in the 1940s, Austrian economists became increasingly critical of mainstream competition models, such as perfect competition and

R. Fillieule, *The Austrian School of Economics*, Palgrave Studies in Austrian Economics,
https://doi.org/10.1007/978-3-031-83414-1_4

monopolistic competition. Kirzner (1973) advanced the Austrian idea of "entrepreneurial competition," combining Hayek's (1948 [1946]) view of competition as a process with Mises' (1998b [1949]) theory of entrepreneurship.

4.1 The Theory of Monopoly Price

4.1.1 Economic and Political Monopolies

Economic monopolies arise from the natural operation of a free market, respecting private property rights and freedom of contract. Political monopolies, on the other hand, benefit from state-granted privileges that restrict or prevent competitors from entering the market through the threat of legal sanctions. This chapter will focus solely on economic monopolies, while political monopolies will be discussed in the context of state intervention (see Chap. 9).

4.1.2 The Relativity of Monopoly

Menger classically defines a monopolist as the sole seller of a particular good. As Reisman (1996) points out, if a good is defined narrowly enough—by quality, location, time of availability, and so on—then almost every producer could be considered an economic monopolist. Menger uses a simple auction scenario, where a monopolist seeks to sell a good to a group of buyers, to illustrate the following: (1) if the monopolist decides to sell a fixed quantity, he cannot set the unit price above a certain limit, and (2) if he sets the price, he cannot sell more than a certain quantity (1976 [1871], pp. 199–210). As Fetter (1915, p. 79) and later Mises (1998a [1944]) observed, monopoly is *relative*, not absolute. The monopolist is still subject to competitive forces, as consumers determine their demand for the monopolized good based on their demand for other goods. Thus, the producers of all these goods, including the monopolist, compete for a share of consumer spending.

4.1.3 Monopolistic Restriction

Although Menger's available concepts were still quite basic, he recognized that monopoly posed a distinct problem for economic analysis in only one specific case: when restricting the quantity sold raised the price enough to increase the monopolist's income. In other words, this occurs when demand is inelastic within that price range. Menger did not use the terms "elasticity" or "inelasticity," as these concepts were introduced later by Marshall (1920 [1890]). Instead, he used a simple numerical example involving a monopolist with 1000 units of a good:

- If the monopolist sells the entire stock, the price per unit will be 6 ounces of silver, resulting in a total revenue of 6000 ounces.
- However, if only 800 units are sold, the price rises to 9 ounces per unit, yielding a total revenue of 7200 ounces.

In this case, where demand is inelastic, it is in the monopolist's interest to sell only 800 units, even if the remaining 200 units are perishable and cannot be sold later. Historically, producers in markets like spices and tobacco have been known to destroy part of their harvest to raise their income by limiting supply.

Menger further explains that if there were two competing producers, each holding half of the 1000 units, neither would have any incentive to reduce their sale by 200 units. In a competitive scenario (without collusion), the entire stock would be sold, whereas in a monopoly, only part of the stock would be sold at a higher price. With inelastic demand, this monopolistic restriction of supply benefits the monopolist by increasing income but harms consumers, who must pay more for the now-scarcer good.

4.1.4 Monopoly Pricing

Menger's work contains all the foundational elements of monopoly price theory. What remains is to elaborate on it, as Fetter (1915) does by distinguishing between "monopoly price" and "competitive price," as well as between inelastic and elastic demand.

In Table 4.1, demand is divided into two parts: (a) an elastic portion when fewer than 4 units are sold, where increasing the number of units sold raises total income, and (b) an inelastic portion when more than 4 units are sold, where gross income declines with additional sales. In the price-quantity range where demand is *elastic*, the monopolist has no incentive to reduce supply, as doing so would lower gross revenue. Here, the competitive price equals the monopoly price, and no supply restriction occurs under monopolization. However, in the price-quantity range where

Table 4.1 Monopoly price and gross income maximization (after Fetter, 1915, p. 82)

Number of units	*Price per unit*	*Gross income*	
1	7	7	Elastic demand
2	6	12	
3	5	15	
4	**4**	**16**	**Maximum gross income**
5	3	15	Inelastic demand
6	2	12	
7	1	7	

demand is *inelastic*, a monopoly price emerges, exceeding the competitive price, because it is in the monopolist's interest to reduce the quantity offered. For instance, if the monopolist has 6 units, it is more profitable to sell only 4 at $4 per unit (the monopoly price). If the 6 units were sold by competing producers, they would be offered at $2 per unit (the competitive price).

It is also clear that if a monopolist finds it more profitable to withhold part of his stock from the market, it is because he made a forecasting error. If he produces 6 units but profits more from selling only 4, he could have saved on production costs—and increased net income—by producing only 4 units. A rational producer sets output to maximize net income. If the profit-maximizing quantity lies on the inelastic portion of the demand curve, he restricts production until demand becomes elastic. If the profit-maximizing quantity lies on the elastic portion of the demand curve, the producer will set a "competitive price."

4.1.5 Types of Economic Monopolies

When categorizing monopolies, Mises (1998a [1944]) moves away from the strict etymological definition of a monopoly as a single producer, adopting a broader view. A monopoly can consist of a *single producer*, several producers collaborating in a *cartel*, or a group of independent producers whose number is restricted by the state (what Rothbard refers to as a *quasi-monopoly*). According to Rothbard, non-state monopolies—which are the focus of this chapter—can be divided into three categories:

1. *Public utilities*: These are *private* producers responsible for local supplies of essential goods like water, electricity, and natural gas. Today, they often function as political monopolies, benefiting from exclusive licenses granted by national or municipal authorities. Before such state interventions, "public utilities" were typically provided by competing companies, though sometimes by companies with an economic monopoly (Mises, 1998a [1944], p. 26).
2. *Bulky goods production*: In cases where transportation costs are high, a local monopoly can form if only one producer operates in a given area.
3. *Natural resources concentrated in limited locations*: Mises cites diamonds as an example of a global monopoly that emerged without government support, as the resource is concentrated in a few locations.

4.1.6 The Nature of Monopoly Income

According to monopoly pricing theory, a monopolist can secure additional income by restricting production when faced with inelastic demand. This monopoly income is the difference between the gross income of the monopolist and the combined gross income that would be generated by multiple producers competing in the same market. Monopoly income reflects the value of the asset or privilege that gives rise to the monopoly. According to Mises, this asset could be a consumer good, a material production factor, labor, a secret technique, or a legal privilege (in the case of a state monopoly or quasi-monopoly). Monopoly income is derived from the monopolist's control over this resource or privilege (Mises, 1998a [1944], p. 6).

Monopoly income differs from entrepreneurial profit: it is attributed to a specific factor and therefore constitutes that factor's income. Entrepreneurial profits and losses stem from uncertainty about the future and do not exist in an evenly rotating economy (see Sect. 3.2.12). In contrast, monopoly gains are independent of future uncertainty and would persist as factor income even in the ERE (Rothbard, 1962, pp. 596–599).

Kirzner (1973, p. 23) offers a more nuanced view. He argues that if an entrepreneur anticipates the potential gains from monopolizing a certain good before others and successfully acquires the entire stock, this income should be viewed in the long term as entrepreneurial profit. In the short term, however, it may appear as monopoly income, derived from the exclusive control of a factor. Thus, the nature of the income depends on the temporal perspective from which it is analyzed.

4.1.7 Systemic Consequences of Monopoly Pricing

What are the broader economic impacts when a monopoly price is established in a market? Imagine an industry with inelastic demand transitioning from a competitive structure to a monopolistic one, perhaps due to a merger or cartelization. Production would then be restricted to create a monopoly price, which raises the monopolist's income. Some specific factors of production—those that cannot be repurposed for producing other goods—would become idle. However, some of the convertible factors, affected by the production cutback, would be freed up for use in other sectors. Their owners would offer these factors in different markets, causing their prices to decrease. In this way, the contraction of the monopolized industry would be accompanied by growth in other industries.

Under competition, as long as profitability remains above average, investment pours in, increasing supply and raising costs (due to higher demand for factors). This process continues until profitability aligns with the average rate. In contrast, monopoly pricing restricts production in the monopolized sector, benefiting the production of other goods and *distorting overall production* in ways that do not reflect consumer preferences (Mises, 1998a [1944]).

4.1.8 Do Monopoly Prices Tend to Replace Competitive Prices?

A common critique of capitalism in the twentieth century was that it was evolving from a system of competitive pricing toward one dominated by monopoly prices. This "monopolistic capitalism," according to critics, would harm consumers while benefiting capitalists, eventually replacing the original competitive system. Mises rejected this idea. He argued that the rise of monopolies was not the result of a natural tendency in capitalism but rather due to increasing state intervention, which granted more monopolistic privileges to incumbent producers through licenses and the formation of national or international cartels. If monopoly prices were a natural outcome of market evolution, Mises suggested, governments would not need to legislate to create such monopolies.

Rothbard (1962, p. 596) argues that it is competitive prices, not monopoly prices, that tend to prevail as capitalism develops. As markets expand and more goods are produced, consumers are offered wider choices. This increased variety allows spending to shift more easily between different goods, making demands more elastic and reducing opportunities for establishing monopoly prices.

4.1.9 Monopoly Price or Alignment with Production Costs?

Reisman (1996, p. 411) points out that consumer goods with inelastic demand are relatively rare, but the situation is different for intermediate goods. For example, a producer might be willing to pay a high price for essential spare parts without which they cannot complete production, making the demand for these parts inelastic. Despite this, intermediate goods like spare parts are typically sold at their production cost—far below what buyers would be willing to pay if these goods became unusually scarce. So why do sellers not exploit this inelastic demand by significantly raising prices?

The answer lies in long-term incentives. If sellers were to restrict production to take advantage of inelastic demand, they would invite competition. New producers would emerge, offering prices close to production costs and likely securing contracts with buyers to guarantee stable prices. Faced with such alternatives, buyers would quickly abandon the original sellers. As Reisman concludes, even with inelastic demand, the upper limit on selling prices is almost always set by the production costs of potential competitors.

4.1.10 Monopoly Pricing: An Illusion?

Although Rothbard provides an extensive explanation of monopoly price theory, he himself rejects the concept, considering it an "illusion" (1962, p. 586). According to him, neither producers nor outside observers can definitively distinguish a monopoly price from a competitive price. Elements such as restricted production, unusually high earnings, or idle resources do not prove that a monopoly price has been set. In a free market, Rothbard argues, there is no way to determine whether a price is monopolistic or competitive. Therefore, such a distinction is meaningless. In a free market, there can only be "free market prices." It is only in cases of state-enforced monopolies or quasi-monopoly privileges that a restrictionist price—one set above the competitive level—can be identified without ambiguity (see Sect. 9.1.7).

4.2 Entrepreneurial Competition

4.2.1 Biological Versus Catallactic Competition

The founders of the Austrian School did not delve deeply into the concept of competition. Menger and Böhm-Bawerk described a market as "competitive" if several participants independently sought the same goods through exchange. Fetter (1915, p. 73) similarly defines competition as "the attempt of two or more persons to get the same thing," following the word's etymological roots.

Mises (1998b [1949], p. 274) offers a more detailed discussion, contrasting "catallactic" competition, which characterizes a market economy, with biological competition. Biological competition refers to the "implacable" struggle between animals for limited resources necessary for survival. In contrast, catallactic competition is a feature of social cooperation within a system based on private property, exchange, and division of labor. Mises defines it as "the striving of individuals to attain the most favorable position in the system of social cooperation," where sellers aim to offer better and cheaper goods, and buyers bid against each other to secure those goods. It is not a fight for survival where the strongest eliminate the weakest, but rather a process of reallocation, where individuals are moved to positions more suited to their actual efficiency. Therefore, biological or military metaphors are inappropriate for understanding catallactic competition.

4.2.2 A Broad Conception of Competition

Catallactic competition is not confined to the market for a single type of good or even to markets for similar goods. Instead, it is a comprehensive process where:

1. Consumers compete for goods and services from companies that produce consumer products, while these companies (downstream) compete for consumer spending.
2. All companies (upstream) compete for investors' capital.
3. Owners of original factors (labor, land) and capital goods compete to sell their resources to firms, which in turn compete to buy them. The broader the convertibility of these factors, the wider the competition; the more specific the factor, the narrower the competition. However, competition is very rarely confined to a single market.

Traditional conceptions of competition, such as the pure and perfect competition model or the monopolistic competition model, are much narrower. These models will be critiqued later, in part, for this limitation.

4.2.3 Competition as a Dynamic Process of Discovery

Hayek (1948 [1946]) introduces a crucial distinction between competition as a process that leads to equilibrium and competition as the outcome of that process. In standard models, a market is deemed to be in a state of "perfect competition" only when it has *reached* its final equilibrium. At this equilibrium, the decisions of all participants align, making it impossible for anyone to introduce genuine innovations or surprise others. Thus, competition as emulation, which reflects real competition with unpredictable outcomes, cannot occur in this state.

It is essential to differentiate between *dynamic competition*—where participants gradually uncover and utilize information to offer better trading terms—and *static competition*, which ultimately results from this discovery process. By focusing exclusively on the mathematical conditions that characterize static competition (i.e., "competitive equilibrium"), traditional economists overlook the phenomenon of dynamic competition, which is vital for understanding how a market economy operates. This dynamic aspect corresponds more closely with the everyday and business meanings of "competition."

4.2.4 The Entrepreneurial Element in Human Action

In the context of dynamic competition, human action cannot be reduced to a mere logical choice in a given framework (Hayek, 1945). At the outset of the process, the system is in a state of disequilibrium, and the plans of various participants are inconsistent. Not all of these plans can be executed as intended; consequently, participants must adjust them by incorporating unanticipated information gained during the process. Kirzner (1973) builds on Hayek's analysis by distinguishing between two fundamentally different aspects of human action. The first is the *maximizing* aspect, which exemplifies the pure logic of choice, or instrumental rationality. Here, the actor uses available means toward desired ends based on known techniques. The second aspect is the *entrepreneurial* dimension, which involves discovering new ends, means, or techniques and being attuned to these possibilities of discovery. Kirzner defines this entrepreneurial element as the actor's *alertness* to the potential for new ends, means, or techniques, allowing for action that is active and creative rather than passive and mechanical (1973, p. 35).

4.2.5 *Entrepreneurial Competition*

In a market process, the entrepreneurial element involves being vigilant to identify better buying and selling opportunities. This alertness to opportunities for purchasing at lower prices and selling at higher prices is what fosters genuine competition; thus, entrepreneurship serves as the driving force behind competitive dynamics. Kirzner concludes that competition (in its dynamic form) and entrepreneurship are *inseparable* concepts, akin to two sides of the same coin. In a state of individual or systemic equilibrium, participants make decisions based on a fixed framework of ends, means, and techniques, leaving no room for either entrepreneurship or competition. It is only when equilibrium is disrupted—when the actions of different participants conflict—that those with entrepreneurial awareness can adjust their plans by identifying new ends, means, or techniques. These adjustments enable them to make offers that better align with the market conditions (for sellers) or to express demands that yield greater satisfaction (for buyers). From this perspective, the market process is defined by both its competitive and its entrepreneurial dimensions.

All participants engage in entrepreneurial alertness: consumers remain alert to new products that may satisfy their needs or opportunities to purchase at lower prices, while owners of production factors seek to sell their resources under more favorable conditions. However, the quintessential form of entrepreneurial activity within the market process is speculative *arbitrage*—buying to resell. This entails acquiring goods to sell them later or elsewhere, or purchasing factors to combine and sell their resulting products. The "pure" entrepreneur, in Kirzner's framework, exercises vigilance to buy low and sell high to make a profit, and should not be conflated with resource owners such as capitalists or managers. If an entrepreneur invests their own funds or operates their own business, it is as if they rented their capital or labor resources to themselves (Salerno, 2008 criticizes this view and contends, in opposition to Kirzner, that resource ownership should not be separated from the entrepreneurial function).

A key aspect of Kirzner's perspective is that entrepreneurial activity is inherently competitive (in the sense of dynamic competition). In the absence of legal barriers to entry, entrepreneurs cannot shield themselves from the competitive activities of others who seek to offer more attractive exchange opportunities than their own.

4.2.6 *Entrepreneurship and Monopoly*

Monopoly inherently opposes competition. However, if, as Kirzner claims, entrepreneurship is "always" competitive, then the market process seems to allow no space for monopoly as long as there is freedom of entry in all markets. Nonetheless, there is one exception that could prevent entrepreneurs from capitalizing on the profit opportunities they discover: the monopolization of a resource. Only through monopolistic control of a resource—or a state-granted monopoly privilege—can a producer partially evade the pressures of dynamic competition. Kirzner illustrates this point by stating, "Without access to oranges, entry into the production of orange juice *is* blocked" (1973, p. 103).

While competitive pressure will still exist between orange juice and other beverages, and even more broadly between beverages and other goods, the producer who monopolizes oranges enjoys a certain degree of protection in the orange juice manufacturing activities. This situation does not contradict the previous argument, as the protection arises not from being a "pure" entrepreneur but from being the owner of a resource. If we consider a monopolist, such as the State, gradually gaining control over more resources, the space available for competitive entrepreneurial processes would diminish until it eventually vanished in a fully collectivized economy.

Kirzner further notes that monopoly, in the sense of resource monopolization, can stem from prior competitive activity (as already seen in Sect. 4.1.6). For instance, if an entrepreneur is the first to recognize that acquiring the entire stock of a resource can generate additional income, and succeeds in monopolizing that resource, then the monopoly arises from entrepreneurial competition. In this case, what appears to be monopoly rent in the short term may be viewed as entrepreneurial profit in the long run.

4.2.7 *Goods Differentiation, Sales Costs, and Advertising*

Standard views of competition often classify product differentiation, sales costs, and advertising as monopolistic phenomena. However, according to Kirzner's theory of entrepreneurial competition, these elements are fundamentally competitive.

Competitiveness Beyond Pricing: Competitiveness, in the sense of striving to provide better exchange opportunities, is not confined to price competition for given types of products. Competitive pressure encompasses, and perhaps primarily involves, the variety and quality of goods offered for sale. Entrepreneurial vigilance helps identify the types of differentiation that buyers desire, specifically new types or qualities of goods that consumers would be willing to pay a premium for, ensuring a profit after accounting for production costs. Thus, the *differentiation of goods and their qualities* is not a monopolistic loophole but a crucial aspect of dynamic competition.

The Distinction Between Production and Sales Costs: Some economists, such as Chamberlin (1956 [1933]), have attempted to distinguish between production costs (related to manufacturing and transporting the product) and sales costs (which aim to increase demand). They have raised concerns about the monopolistic risks associated with increasing these sales costs. However, Kirzner argues that this distinction is arbitrary because entrepreneurial activity is not about producing a product and then trying to sell it: *the primary goal is selling*. All expenses incurred by the entrepreneur can be viewed as a single category, encompassing exclusively selling costs. As Mises (1998b [1949], p. 319) noted, there is no scientific basis for differentiating between the socially useful activity of production and the potentially unproductive activity of marketing within the dynamic market process.

Advertising as a Tool of Competition: Advertising is perhaps the most well-known and debated aspect of sales efforts. In the standard model of perfect competition, advertising is useless since consumers are assumed to be fully informed. However, in a dynamic and uncertain environment where entrepreneurs strive to introduce consumers to new goods or qualities, advertising is not limiting competition. Rather, it is one of the essential tools of competitive rivalry. If advertising often comes across as flashy and provocative, it is because entrepreneurs must go beyond simply presenting product information to consumers; they need to *consistently remind consumers of its existence*.

4.2.8 Critique of "Perfect Competition"

Competition in the market for a homogeneous good is deemed "perfect" when each participant is small enough not to influence price-setting, there are no legal barriers to entry, and all players possess perfect information. Under these conditions, the model concludes that at market equilibrium, the selling price of the product is unique and equal to both its marginal

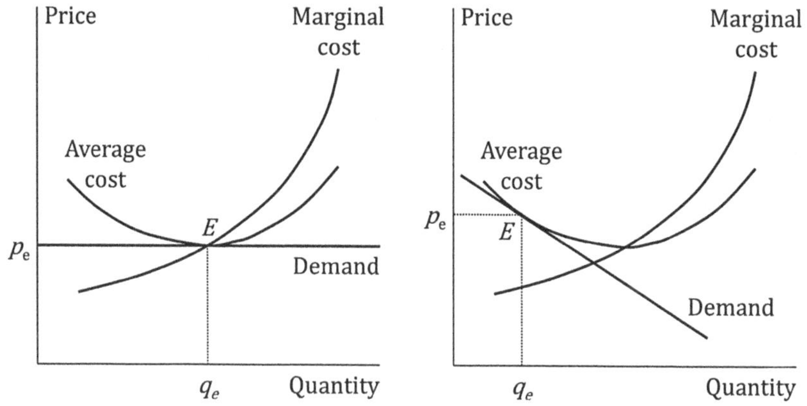

Fig. 4.1 Market equilibrium in perfect competition (*left*) and in monopolistic competition (*right*)

cost (the cost required for a firm to produce one additional unit of the good) and its minimum average cost (cost per unit). In this context, each firm's average cost versus quantity produced curve is assumed to decline to a minimum and then rise again (see Fig. 4.1 and any standard textbook, for instance, Mankiw, 2010). Austrian economists fundamentally reject this model for several reasons.

Mises (1998a [1944], p. 12) criticizes the model as overly simplistic. He argues that competition cannot be confined to a single market; a company competes not only by lowering its prices relative to others offering the same product but also by providing different types of goods. Each well-known singer or actor delivers a unique service, which is precisely what makes them competitive—not only against other singers or actors but also against all other types of goods that consumers might purchase (books, clothes, etc.). He further points out that if a firm does not expand its production until the selling price equals marginal cost, this does not imply it is engaging in monopolistic behavior; rather, it indicates that the final equilibrium of the economic system has not yet been achieved. In both monopoly and monopolistic competition models, firms are incentivized to restrict production in equilibrium to keep the selling price above marginal cost. Since such an equilibrium cannot realistically occur due to frequent unanticipated dynamic shocks, it is inappropriate to use it as a normative benchmark. The positive difference between unit price and average cost (including interest) represents an entrepreneurial profit that is only temporary and will diminish as the firm or industry develops.

Hayek (1948 [1946]) emphasizes the issue of information acquisition. The model of perfect competition assumes that players already possess the information that dynamic competition has helped uncover: (a) what goods consumers demand and (b) how to produce these goods at the lowest cost. Hayek finds it paradoxical to label competition as "perfect" when the most competitive activities—such as advertising, cost-cutting, and product differentiation—are rendered irrelevant. Another challenge with this model arises from the assumption of product homogeneity; no two companies produce exactly the same good. Moreover, Hayek argues that, as a normative ideal, perfect competition sets an excessively demanding criterion. What we can realistically expect from competition is merely a tendency to discover consumer preferences and to meet their needs at progressively lower costs and prices.

Rothbard (1962, p. 633) defines perfect competition in terms of a horizontal demand function (perfectly elastic demand), indicating that each firm is negligible in size relative to the market and cannot influence the market price of the good. He stresses the unrealistic nature of this model aspect; in reality, demand can never be perfectly horizontal. Any increase, no matter how small, in the quantity produced leads to a decrease in price, implying that every company has some influence on the selling price.

Reisman (1996) critiques the normative implications of the perfect competition model. If setting the selling price at the level of marginal cost is considered an ideal of efficiency, many firms would have to price their goods below their average unit costs. For instance, the marginal costs of certain activities can be very low or even zero—such as for companies whose factories are underutilized, rail or airline companies with empty seats, theaters, etc. To adhere to this alleged efficiency criterion, these firms would have to operate at a loss. As a result, they would require subsidies to stay afloat, and the funds raised by the state to provide these subsidies would reduce production in other sectors, causing inefficiency and waste.

4.2.9 Critique of "Monopolistic Competition"

In the 1930s, Chamberlin (1956 [1933]) and Robinson (1933) developed the models of "monopolistic competition" and "imperfect competition," two closely related theories that describe a market structure situated between perfect competition and monopoly. These models are said to represent the most common scenario in a developed capitalist economy.

Chamberlin's concept of monopolistic competition involves numerous firms selling similar yet slightly differentiated products. These firms are in "competition" due to their numbers and the freedom to enter the market, while simultaneously possessing a "monopoly" because each firm offers a unique product. This differentiation leads to a downward-sloping demand curve for each firm, in contrast to the horizontal demand curve found in perfect competition. The average cost curve (as a function of the quantity produced) is assumed to be U-shaped, initially decreasing and then increasing (this is because, as production increases, average fixed costs decrease while average variable costs increase). In a state of market equilibrium, a perfectly competitive firm maximizes its profit by producing the quantity that aligns with the minimum average cost, thereby producing goods as efficiently as possible. In contrast, a monopolistically competitive firm aims to produce a quantity that is less than what would correspond to its minimum average cost, due to its downward-sloping demand curve. Consequently, it does not operate at the most economical point in terms of cost. Compared to a purely competitive firm, a monopolistically competitive firm restricts its production and raises its selling price (see Fig. 4.1), which makes it less efficient from an economic standpoint.

Austrian economists are equally critical of this theory as they are of the model of perfect competition.

Mises (1998a [1944]) defines "imperfect" competition as a scenario where a company does not utilize its equipment to full capacity, even though doing so would lower its average cost. He argues that this situation does not necessarily indicate that the company is engaging in monopolistic practices. To operate at full capacity, the firm would need to acquire additional factors of production, which would be diverted from other sectors. If those other sectors are yielding higher profits, this implies stronger demand for their products. While acquiring these additional factors might lower the company's average costs, it would disrupt the market by reallocating resources from the sectors that consumers value more.

Hayek (1948 [1946], p. 94) does not provide a specific analysis of monopolistic competition. Instead, he asserts that his critiques of perfect competition also apply to monopolistic competition, a point that Kirzner later elaborates on (see below).

Rothbard (1962) addresses the theoretical distinction between perfect and monopolistic competition. He posits that a demand function is always decreasing and argues that perfect competition cannot truly exist. Thus, he believes there is little value in contrasting it with monopolistic competition or using it as a normative benchmark. Rothbard also maintains that product differentiation is not merely a tactic employed by producers but a genuine method for better satisfying the diverse needs of consumers.

The theory of monopolistic competition aims to provide a more realistic depiction of how the economic system operates compared to the theory of perfect competition, largely due to its inclusion of significant factors such as product differentiation and sales efforts. However, Kirzner (1973), developing the Hayekian perspective, argues that the monopolistic competition model fails to address the shortcomings of the perfect competition model, as it suffers from the same fundamental flaws. Both models presume that producers have ***already identified*** their cost functions and the demand for their products. This foundational assumption indicates a disregard for the entrepreneurial competition process that led to the discovery of this information, thus evading the critical issue of how such data is obtained.

Regarding product differentiation, the monopolistic competition theory assumes that at equilibrium, each producer offers a unique product. However, if market entry is unrestricted, why would producers not simply replicate the goods that consumers desire? Since no resources are presumed to be monopolized, there is nothing preventing firms from imitating the most efficient producer. Consequently, this theory cannot adequately explain the very phenomenon of differentiation that it starts with. According to Kirzner, product differentiation results from choices made by entrepreneurs, who employ their vigilance to uncover the most attractive opportunities for consumers. In summary, the theory of monopolistic competition fails to account for the essential aspects of dynamic competition and mistakenly equates product differentiation with a form of monopoly. This misunderstanding leads Kirzner to label it a "decidedly unfortunate episode in the history of modern economic thought" (1973, p. 114).

References

Chamberlin, E. H. (1956 [1933]). *The Theory of Monopolistic Competition* (7th ed.). Harvard University Press.

Fetter, F. (1915). *Economic Principles.* Century.

Hayek, F. A. (1945). The Use of Knowledge in Society. *American Economic Review, 35*(4), 519–530.

Hayek, F. A. (1948 [1946]). The Meaning of Competition. In F. A. Hayek (Ed.), *Individualism and Economic Order* (pp. 92–106). The University of Chicago Press.

Kirzner, I. M. (1973). *Competition and Entrepreneurship.* The University of Chicago Press.

Mankiw, G. N. (2010). *Principles of Economics.* Cengage Learning.

Marshall, A. (1920 [1890]). *Principles of Economics. An Introductory Volume.* Macmillan.

Menger, C. (1976 [1871]). *Principles of Economics.* New York University Press.

Reisman, G. (1996). *Capitalism. A Treatise on Economics.* Jameson Books.

Robinson, J. (1933). *The Economics of Imperfect Competition.* Macmillan.

Rothbard, M. N. (1962). *Man, Economy, and State. A Treatise on Economic Principles.* D. Van Nostrand.

Salerno, J. T. (2008). The Entrepreneur: Real and Imagined. *Quarterly Journal of Austrian Economics, 11*, 188–207.

von Mises, L. (1998a [1944]). Monopoly Prices. *Quarterly Journal of Austrian Economics, 1*(2), 1–28.

von Mises, L. (1998b [1949]). *Human Action. A Treatise on Economics.* Ludwig von Mises Institute.

CHAPTER 5

Production and Time

Abstract This chapter explores key concepts such as diminishing returns, capital accumulation, economic progress, and the structure of production. It examines Böhm-Bawerk's idea that roundaboutness—extending production time—enhances productivity. Hayek's triangle is introduced to illustrate the multi-stage production process. Additionally, the chapter critiques the standard aggregate of the Gross Domestic Product as an insufficient measure of economic activity and refutes the Keynesian "paradox of saving," emphasizing savings as a driver of long-term economic growth and wealth creation.

Keywords Diminishing returns • Roundaboutness • Production structure • Hayek's Triangle

The foundations of Austrian production theory were established by Böhm-Bawerk (1959 [1889]) with his concept of the "roundabout" production process, in which capital accumulation extends the overall duration of production, requiring more time to produce the final consumer goods—a disadvantage balanced by the ability to get consumer goods in larger quantities or of higher quality. Hayek (1931) introduced a graphical representation of this structure of production in the form of a triangle,

R. Fillieule, *The Austrian School of Economics*, Palgrave Studies in Austrian Economics,
https://doi.org/10.1007/978-3-031-83414-1_5

illustrating the sequence of stages and capital accumulation. This primary model of Austrian macroeconomics was later expanded by Rothbard (1962), Skousen (1990), Reisman (1996), Huerta de Soto (2006 [1998]), and Garrison (2001).

5.1 The Laws of Production

5.1.1 *Production as a Material Process*

Böhm-Bawerk (1959 [1889]) approaches the concept of production by adopting an idea rooted in Classical economics: the production of a material good is not the creation of something new but rather the rearrangement of pre-existing matter. The processes involved in producing material goods revolve around harnessing natural forces to manipulate matter, either by moving it (transport), altering its form (shaping), or combining it (assembly). Fetter (1915) categorizes these processes into four types: changes in substance (e.g., cooking, fermentation, ripening), changes in form (e.g., weaving, carpentry), changes in location (physical movement of objects), and changes in time (e.g., bringing forward the availability of a good, as in agriculture with greenhouses, or delaying it through techniques like refrigeration or vacuum preservation).

5.1.2 *Production as Action*

Taking a step beyond the physical description of production processes, Mises (1998 [1949], pp. 140–142) views all human action as a form of production, as it always involves the combination of various factors—such as labor and land—to produce a desired outcome. From this standpoint, there is no reason to classify certain actions or factors as inherently productive while dismissing others. The French Physiocrats of the eighteenth century were mistaken in their belief that only agriculture, fishing, hunting, and mining were productive, and that artisanal and commercial activities were "sterile." Similarly, Classical economists were wrong to label personal services such as a doctor's prescription as "unproductive" in comparison to the manufacturing of material goods. Contemporary economists continue to make similar errors when they disparage marketing and advertising as unproductive. According to Mises, the "essential requisites" of production are not found in its material components or techniques, but in the decision to act. Unlike Marx, Mises explicitly argues that the true productive forces are not material, but spiritual, intellectual, and ideological.

5.1.3 The Law of Diminishing Returns

Discovered in the early nineteenth century by Malthus and Ricardo about agriculture, this law was regarded by John Stuart Mill as "the most important proposition in political economy" (1987 [1848], p. 177). Mises places it second only to the law of marginal utility among the fundamental laws of human action. He provides a detailed explanation and proof (1998 [1949], pp. 127–129), as do Rothbard (1962, p. 30) and Reisman (1996, p. 67).

The law of returns states that in any production process, if the quantity of one factor (the *variable* factor) increases while the quantities of complementary factors (the *fixed* factors) remain constant, the productivity of the variable factor (i.e., the total quantity produced divided by the quantity of the variable factor) will eventually decrease, assuming all other conditions remain equal. This diminishing return implies that there is a certain quantity of the variable factor—known as the *optimum*—at which the return reaches its maximum.

Mises demonstrates this law through a reductio ad absurdum argument. He imagines a production process to which the law does not apply. The result would be that unlimited quantities of goods could be produced even if a fixed factor was reduced to an infinitesimally small level, provided the variable factors were increased sufficiently (e.g., producing enough food for the entire human population on a tiny plot of land, as long as enough labor and capital were applied). This would imply that the productivity of the variable factors is infinite, more than compensating for an extremely small amount of the fixed factor. This is absurd, and therefore the law of diminishing returns must hold true. Moreover, it applies not only to agriculture, where it was first discovered, but universally to all production processes.

5.1.4 Consequences of Diminishing Returns and Counteracting Forces

Classical economists had already identified one of the major consequences of the law of diminishing returns: given a fixed amount of agricultural land (a fixed factor), an increase in population—and thus in the number of workers (the variable factor)—will eventually lead, all else being equal, to a decline in the average productivity of agricultural labor. This decline will in turn result in a reduction in the average standard of living. Reisman (1996, p. 70) further notes that as natural resources are depleted (e.g., requiring deeper extraction), even if the population remains constant, the standard of living will tend to decline due to diminishing returns in resource extraction.

More broadly, the law of diminishing returns illustrates the limits to economic progress when a factor of production, such as land or any other higher-order good, is fixed and cannot be increased. However, forces can offset the effects of diminishing returns:

1. The discovery and adoption of more efficient production techniques (or the discovery of new resource-rich deposits),
2. The intensification of the division of labor,
3. Capital accumulation through increased savings.

5.1.5 *Technical Progress*

According to Menger (1976 [1871], p. 74), in contrast to Adam Smith's view, the primary driver of economic progress is not the intensification of the division of labor, but rather the advancement of knowledge about natural phenomena. As the causal relationships between these phenomena are better understood, it becomes possible to implement more efficient production processes by preparing the necessary materials, tools, or machines in advance. As a result, labor can produce more and higher-quality goods. The human economy evolves from merely collecting consumer goods scattered throughout the environment to utilizing controlled production processes that achieve their goals with significant assistance from the forces of nature.

Menger also notes that technological progress leads to the use of increasingly higher-order goods, adding additional upstream stages to the production process. However, it is important to distinguish between these two elements: technical progress and the extension of the production structure. As Böhm-Bawerk acknowledges, certain technological advancements can actually shorten the production structure. Similarly, economic actors may choose to reduce the number of production stages in order to save time, even if they are aware of more productive techniques that would require a longer lead time. Furthermore, the multiplication of production stages—such as the prefabrication of tools, machines, or buildings—is one form of the division of labor, specifically the *vertical* division of labor (Hayek, 1941, pp. 71–73).

5.1.6 *Division of Labor and Society*

The Austrian School of Economics has always recognized the importance of the division of labor, but Mises (1981 [1922], pp. 258–276) was the first to explore the concept in depth. For him, the division of labor is of immense importance, as it forms the foundation of human society. Individuals realize that by specializing in the tasks they are most skilled at, they can collectively increase overall production, compared to a situation where each person tries to meet all their own needs independently. Acting in their own self-interest, people naturally form cooperative relationships based on this division of labor. If they did not recognize that specialization enhances productivity, or if, hypothetically, it did not lead to greater output, Mises argues that human society would not exist. The rise of extended societies cannot be attributed to an assumed instinct to gather in groups, as this would imply that people form societies simply because they have an innate drive to do so—a circular and unscientific argument.

Society is simply a cooperative mechanism that enables individuals to better satisfy their various needs. Its development or decline depends on whether the division of labor intensifies or disintegrates.

Rothbard (1962, p. 80) explains that an individual's decision to specialize in a particular field of production depends on several factors: available natural resources, amounts and qualities of capital goods, personal skills, and preferences between different activities.

5.1.7 *Division of Labor and Production*

Mises (1998 [1949], p. 157) highlights three consequences of the division of labor: the geographical distribution of productive activities, the differentiation of individuals' productive abilities according to their specialization, and the use of machines. Reisman (1996, p. 123) provides a more detailed analysis, identifying six key advantages that the division of labor brings to production:

1. *Multiplication of knowledge*: In a society with a high degree of specialization, the knowledge developed in each specific field combines into a vast pool of expertise, vastly outstripping the limited, generalized knowledge found in less-specialized societies, where individuals often share the same skills.

2. *Benefit from geniuses*: Great scientists and inventors can dedicate themselves entirely to advancing knowledge and technology.
3. *Concentration on individuals' advantages*: People can focus on the tasks best suited to their physical or intellectual abilities, allowing production to benefit from absolute or comparative advantages.
4. *Geographical specialization*: Different regions are better suited to certain types of production due to factors like land, climate, and natural resources. Through the division of labor and trade, regions can share their surpluses and benefit from one another's strengths, such as using energy resources from one area to fuel agricultural or mining activities in another.
5. *Economies of learning and motion*: Repetition of specific tasks and techniques increases productivity and makes learning more efficient, reducing the time spent acquiring skills relative to the time spent applying them. In factories, the division of labor minimizes unnecessary movements, enhancing overall efficiency.
6. *Use of machinery*: Specialization allows for the use and development of machines, from their design (thanks to specialized inventors) to sourcing materials globally, efficient assembly in factories, and profitable use through mass production.

Reisman also emphasizes the critical role of capitalism's major institutions in establishing, intensifying, and rationalizing the division of labor. These institutions include private property, trade and money, savings and capital accumulation, competition and income inequality, and coordination through market prices.

5.1.8 The Law of Roundaboutness

Central to Böhm-Bawerk's theory of production is the law of roundabout production, a concept first introduced by Menger in the analysis of *capital accumulation*. Imagine villagers who need to collect water from a nearby river. They could scoop it up with their hands, which is the most direct method. Alternatively, they could spend time making containers, allowing them to carry larger amounts of water per trip. Although this method increases the duration of the overall process—because they need time to make the buckets—the productivity of their labor improves. Lastly, they could build a water conveyance system, such as a network of pipes, which would take even longer to construct but would provide them with much larger quantities of water where and when needed.

Böhm-Bawerk generalizes this example, stating that more "roundabout" methods of production are typically more productive than direct methods for creating consumer goods (1959 [1889], p. 12). A method is considered more "roundabout" or indirect when labor and natural resources are spread over a longer period, thereby extending the overall production time. This lengthening of time between the start of the process and the final appearance of consumer goods allows for greater quantities, better quality, or goods that simply could not be produced with shorter production methods.

The law of roundabout production, therefore, highlights the temporal aspect of productive processes. It shows that the same amount of labor, when applied over a longer period, can yield a greater quantity of consumer goods per unit of time or produce goods that cannot be made within a shorter timeframe. In other words, the "detour" increases the quantities produced or improves quality without the need for more labor. However, Mises (1998 [1949], p. 478) critiques the term "detour," arguing that individuals choose these indirect production methods because they represent the most efficient path to achieving their goals of enhancing the quantity or quality of production.

5.1.9 The Intertemporal Production Function

Böhm-Bawerk applies the law of diminishing returns to roundabout production. The increase in production from these more extended production processes diminishes with the length of the process. While Böhm-Bawerk does not specify this explicitly, it can be inferred that the fixed factor is the amount of labor, as natural resources are continually recovered in larger quantities, as explained in Sect. 5.1.10. Wicksell (1954 [1893], p. 122) represents this intertemporal production function with the curve shown in Fig. 5.1: the quantity of consumer goods (Q_t) produced per unit of time increases as the duration (d) of the production process lengthens (law of roundaboutness), but at a diminishing rate (law of returns).

Fig. 5.1 The intertemporal production function (after Wicksell, 1954 [1893], p. 122)

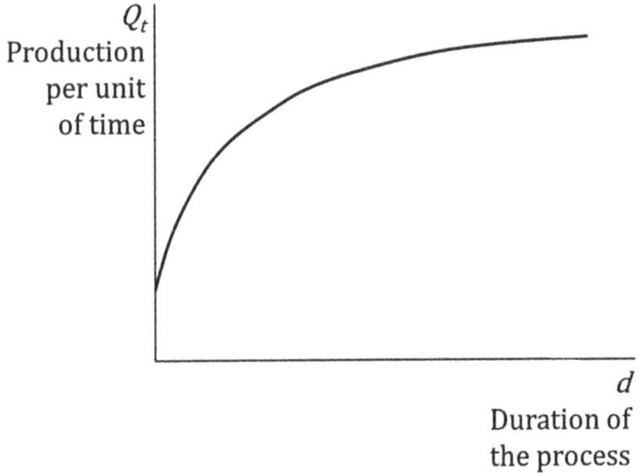

5.1.10 Explaining the Productivity of the Roundabout Process

The law of the production "detour" does not claim that any extension of the production process is automatically productive, but rather that certain *carefully chosen* extensions can enhance productivity. For Böhm-Bawerk, this law is "purely technical" and can be explained by the fact that a "detour" allows additional natural forces to be incorporated into the production process. For instance, using a bucket enables us to harness the natural properties that make the container watertight and rigid, allowing us to transport larger quantities of water. Hayek (1941, p. 60) adds that certain delays in the process are necessary to fully leverage the power of certain natural forces and resources. The longer the "detour," the more powerful these forces become, and the more resources can be accessed. As the production process lengthens, new types of resources become available, transforming into factors of production. Importantly, Hayek (1936) emphasizes that the productivity of the "detour" applies to a given level of knowledge and does not require any technological advances. Technical progress shifts the curve in Fig. 5.1 upward.

5.1.11 Saving-Investment

Direct methods of production, such as foraging or picking, are not highly productive. Individuals can extend the production process to increase both the quantity and quality of the products. However, implementing the "detour" requires reallocating some labor to the earlier stages of production. Two scenarios are then possible: either the total labor supply remains unchanged, in which case the production of consumer goods will temporarily decrease because part of the labor previously used in the final stages is diverted, or the total labor supply increases because individuals sacrifice leisure time to contribute more to production. In both cases, a temporary *sacrifice of present goods* is endured, which represents savings and investment and is aimed at increasing future consumption. Individuals must decide whether the anticipated increase in future consumption justifies the immediate sacrifice. This decision is influenced by factors such as their preference for present consumption, the availability of capital and consumer goods, and the relative efficiency of various known production methods.

5.1.12 Measuring the Production Period?

Böhm-Bawerk proposes that, instead of measuring the total production period of a process, we should focus on its *average* period (1959 [1889], pp. 86–87). Every product we use today is the result of a long series of production processes spanning centuries. The total production period is therefore of little practical relevance. Instead, he seeks to account for the fact that the labor performed far in the past has only a minimal impact on the current product, as it represents only a very small fraction of the total labor involved. To provide a more meaningful understanding of the process's duration, Böhm-Bawerk suggests calculating the average production period. For example, if a process required a quantity q_3 of labor 3 years ago, q_2 2 years ago, q_1 1 year ago, and q_0 at the final stage, the average production period can be calculated using his formula:

$$\frac{3q_3 + 2q_2 + 1q_1 + 0q_0}{q_3 + q_2 + q_1 + q_0}$$

Mises (1998 [1949], p. 477) criticized the concept of the average production period, arguing that it is retroactive and disconnected from the forward-looking nature of human action. Hayek (1941, p. 141) further highlights the oversimplification of this measure. In more complex and realistic scenarios, it is impossible to combine the varying durations of the many processes that make up the economic system into a single, unified measure of the system's overall production period.

5.2 The Macroeconomics of the Production Structure

5.2.1 *The Hayekian Production Structure*

Böhm-Bawerk (1959 [1889], p. 106) provided an early graphic representation of the overall production structure, using concentric circles to depict different "maturity classes" of capital goods. However, we can set aside his diagram, as Hayek's (1931) model, originally in Jevons (1965 [1871], p. 230), is far more insightful. Before delving into Hayek's "triangle," it is helpful to revisit the concept of the production structure itself. The consumer goods produced in any given year are the result of a process that began several years earlier. Figure 5.2 illustrates a simplified economic system in which the entire production process occurs over *four successive stages*, each lasting *1 year*, and numbered from the stage closest to final consumption to the stage furthest away. During these four stages, the original factors of labor and land are gradually transformed into final consumer goods.

5.2.2 *The Hayekian Triangle*

Hayek's triangle (1931) can now be represented using a more comprehensive version, later developed by Rothbard (1962, p. 314). The production structure is divided into *six stages*, each lasting *one year* (see

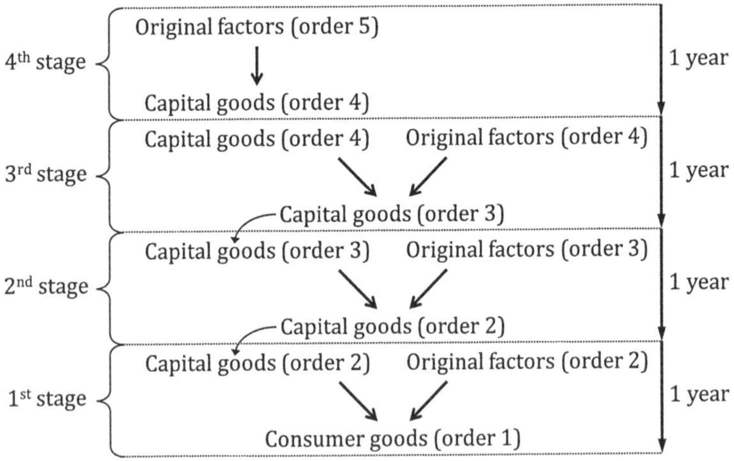

Fig. 5.2 Illustration of a 4-stage production structure

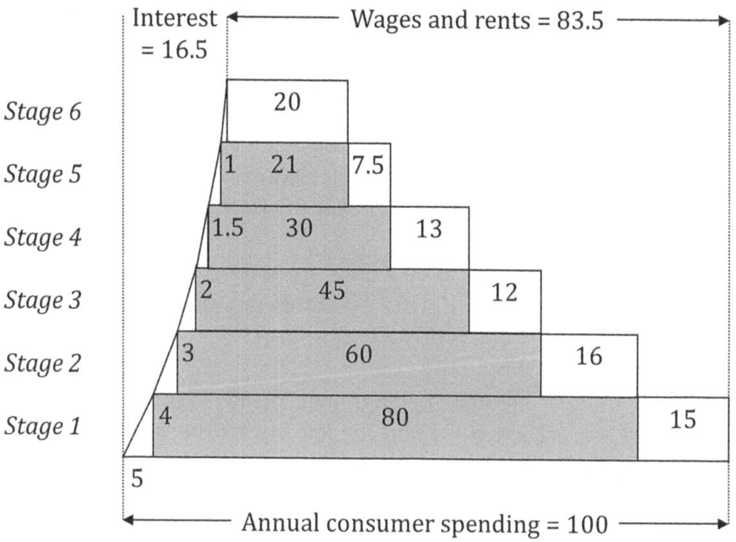

Fig. 5.3 Rothbard's diagram of the production structure (adapted from Rothbard, 1962, p. 314)

Fig. 5.3). In this model, capital goods (produced factors of production) are represented by gray rectangles, while original factors (labor and land) are shown as white rectangles on the right-hand side. Rothbard also accounts for interest payments, represented as white triangles on the left-hand side of the structure. The annual interest rate is assumed to be 5%. The production structure is described below, moving backward through the stages, starting from the final stage that produces consumer goods:

1. *Stage 1*: The annual value of consumer goods produced is assumed to be 100 monetary units. With an interest rate of 5%, the initial investment for stage 1 (1 year earlier) is calculated using the equation $I_1(1 + 0.05) = 100$, which gives $I_1 = 95$ (rounded). Interest income for this stage is $100 - 95 = 5$ monetary units. The price of the original factors used at this stage is arbitrarily assumed to be 15.
2. *Stage 2*: This stage produces the capital goods used in stage 1, valued at 80 units (calculated as $I_1 - 15 = 95 - 15$). The investment at the start of stage 2 is determined by $I_2\,(1 + 0.05) = 80$, resulting in $I_2 = 76$ (rounded). Interest income for this stage is $80 - 76 = 4$

monetary units. The price of the original factors used at this stage is arbitrarily assumed to be 16.

3. *Subsequent stages*: By knowing the interest rate, the number of stages, and arbitrarily setting the aggregate price for the original factors in each stage (15 for stage 1, 16 for stage 2, 12 for stage 3, 13 for stage 4, and 7.5 for stage 5), similar calculations can be applied to move through each stage until the entire production structure is determined.

The production process as a whole spans 6 years, with consumers making a total annual expenditure of 100 monetary units, which represents the value added. This value is divided as follows:

- Annual interest income (or aggregate profit): 16.5 monetary units (= 5 + 4 + 3 + 2 + 1.5 + 1) on the left side of the structure.
- Annual income from the original factors of labor and land (aggregate wage and rent): 83.5 units (= 15 + 16 + 12 + 13 + 7.5 + 20) on the right side of the structure.

5.2.3 *Two Perspectives on the Structure: Synchronic and Diachronic*

In this example, the entire production process takes 6 years, during which labor and land (the original factors) are combined to produce intermediate goods that will eventually be transformed into consumer goods. Does this mean we have to wait 6 years before we can consume anything? No, because in the economic system, production processes are "synchronized," as Clark (1899) explains. Six identical processes run in parallel, each staggered by 1 year, allowing one process to finish *each year*. This ensures a continuous flow of consumer goods.

In any given year, the available original factors are allocated across the various stages of production. For instance, in Rothbard's example, 15 units of original factors are applied in stage 1, 16 in stage 2, 12 in stage 3, and so on. Figure 5.4 illustrates the two possible interpretations of Rothbard's triangle:

1. *Diachronic perspective*: A description of how a single production process unfolds over time, from beginning to end.
2. *Synchronic perspective*: A "snapshot" or cross-section of the economic system in a single year, showing all production processes occurring simultaneously, from those nearing completion to those just beginning, and everything in between.

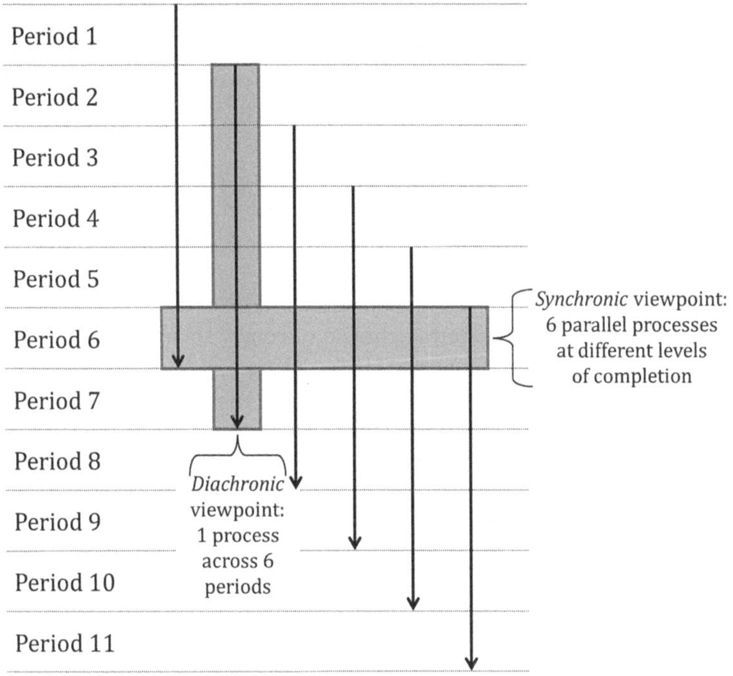

Fig. 5.4 The diachronic and synchronic perspectives in a 6-stage process

The synchronic view is the most valuable as it provides a comprehensive representation of the economic system in a given year.

5.2.4 *Saving and Maintaining the Structure*

This illustration of the production structure helps clarify the criticisms made by Austrian economists (e.g., Hayek, 1936) against the American School represented by Clark and Knight. The latter argue that production and consumption are not only synchronized but also *simultaneous*. They further contend that capital functions as a *perpetual* fund: once capital is formed, its reproduction is no longer an economic issue but merely a "technological detail" (Knight, 1934, p. 259). Figures 5.3 and 5.4 demonstrate that both of these assertions are incorrect.

Firstly, *production and consumption are not simultaneous*. The annual flow of consumer goods (with a total value of 100) results from a process that began 6 years ago and is now finally reaching "maturity." The intermediate stages of transformation (stages 2 to 6) do not allow for consumption, as each stage must wait until the entire process concludes—1 year for stage 2, 2 years for stage 3, and so on. The synchronization of six processes running in parallel does not imply that production and consumption occur simultaneously. Not only does the synchronization of production not eliminate the temporal dimension, but it is the very fact that production takes time that necessitates this synchronization to ensure an uninterrupted flow of consumer goods.

Secondly, *capital is not a perpetual fund*. The structure can only be sustained if capitalists consistently choose to renew their savings each year to fully finance the various stages (Hayek, 1931, p. 48). Each stage represents what Rothbard (1962) refers to as a "time market," where capitalists invest a certain amount (e.g., 60 + 16 in stage 2) and wait a year before receiving their gross income (80) and net income (80 – [60 + 16] = 4), which corresponds to the interest on their capital investment. For the structure to reproduce itself, *all* these time markets (there are six in Fig. 5.3) must secure the necessary savings and investments *each year*, totaling 20 + (21 + 7.5) + (30 + 13) + (45 + 12) + (60 + 16) + (80 + 15) = 319.5 currency units. The reproduction of the structure relies on the decisions of economic agents—in this case, the capitalists' choice not to reduce their overall savings—and is therefore not an automatic process nor a mere "technological detail."

5.2.5 What Is the Total Output? Critique of the GDP

The most commonly used statistical measure for assessing a country's total production is Gross Domestic Product (GDP), which is intended to capture the wealth produced within a single year. However, Rothbard (1962, p. 343) argues, based on his representation of the production structure, that GDP is actually a measure of *net* output rather than gross output.

In the economic system depicted in Fig. 5.3, the annual nominal GDP is 100 monetary units. According to the standard formula, GDP is calculated as GDP = $C + I + G + XN$. In this case, however, there is no investment in durable goods ($I = 0$), government expenditure is assumed to be either zero or included within consumption (C), and there is no foreign trade ($XN = 0$). Consequently, GDP simplifies to annual consumption: GDP = C. This means that GDP statistics only account for the production of consumer goods, entirely disregarding the production of intermediate goods from stages 2 to 6.

Austrian economists argue that the *entire* economic structure should be considered to calculate the true total product, rather than relying solely on GDP. When measured in currency units, this total product therefore includes the outputs from all stages: the output from stage 6 (21 currency units), stage 5 (30), stage 4 (45), and so on, culminating with stage 1 (100). Therefore, the total nominal product amounts to (21 + 30 + 45 + 60 + 80 + 100) = 336 currency units. As a result, standard GDP represents only about 30% of the total product, calculated as (100 ÷ 336) ≈ 0.30. Skousen (1990, p. 191) proposes referring to this total product as GDO (Gross Domestic Output), which significantly exceeds GDP and more accurately reflects overall economic activity.

A common argument in favor of GDP is that when flour is then used to make bread, the price of flour is already incorporated into the price of bread. Thus, adding the two prices together would lead to double counting and overestimating the GDP, with flour being counted twice. Reisman's response (1996, p. 674) is that the economic system produced the flour *and* the bread; therefore, to determine the total product, we cannot treat the system as having produced only the bread. As shown in Fig. 5.5, during period 4, flour is clearly part of the output. Both goods—flour and bread—must be included in the calculation of the gross product. Note that, in this example, wheat is considered an original, unproduced factor, and therefore is not part of the output.

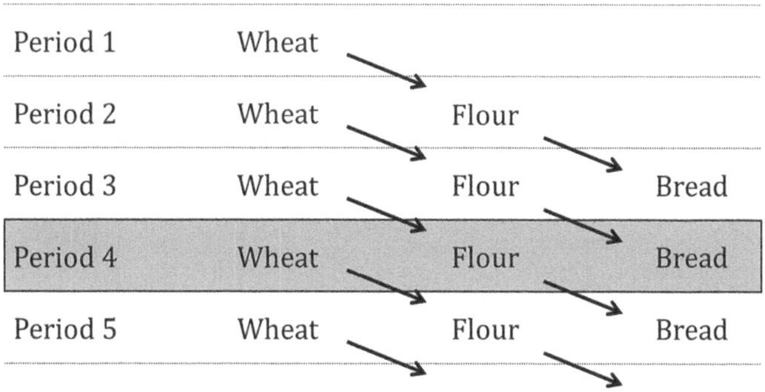

Fig. 5.5 Flour, although an intermediate good, is part of the gross output in each period (adapted from Reisman, 1996, p. 675)

5.2.6 *A Production Structure with Durable Goods*

Austrian economists primarily focus on the type of production structure described above. They tend to emphasize the significance of "circulating capital," which consists of intermediate goods, rather than "fixed capital" (Hayek, 1941, p. 47). In these structures, unproduced natural resources (referred to as "land") are gradually transformed by labor into consumer goods, with capital goods representing the intermediate stages of this transformation process. The lifespan of capital goods does not exceed the duration of one stage (e.g., 1 year), meaning that durable goods are not included in this model.

Hayek (1941, p. 131) presents the contrasting case of a structure composed entirely of durable goods—goods that provide consumption services over several successive periods. In Fig. 5.6, each year, the original factors of labor and land are allocated to produce a durable good that provides consumption services valued at 20 monetary units for 5 years before becoming completely unusable. Here, production is synchronized:

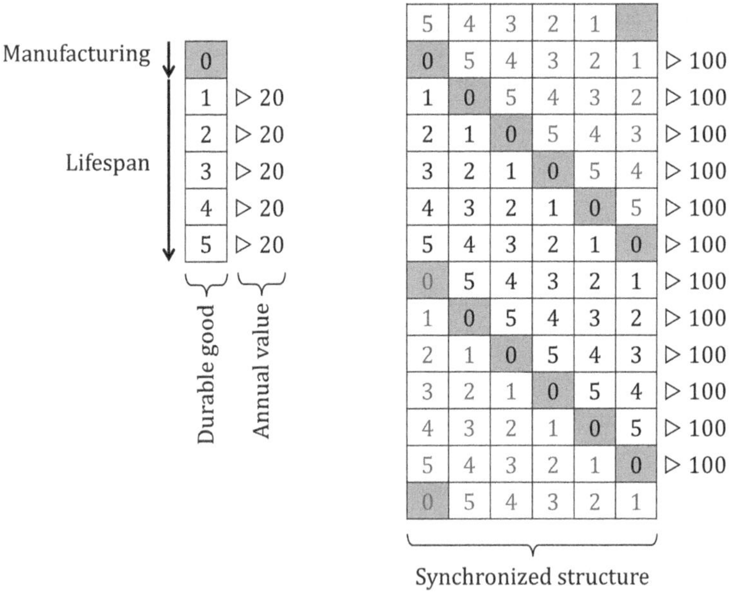

Fig. 5.6 Production structure with durable goods (adapted from Hayek, 1941, p. 131)

the annual flow of consumer goods remains constant, as five durable goods provide their services simultaneously, yielding a total annual value of 5 × 20 = 100 monetary units. These goods are produced with a one-year lag, and as soon as one durable good reaches the end of its lifespan and disappears, 1 year's worth of labor is devoted to replacing it.

In reality, economic systems are complex combinations that integrate multiple entangled stages, encompassing both structures with intermediate non-durable goods and those with durable goods.

5.2.7 *Capital Accumulation*

The Hayekian triangle can effectively illustrate capital accumulation as a more roundabout production process (Hayek, 1931, p. 52). Let us assume that economic actors choose to reduce their consumption in favor of saving and investing, prompted by a decrease in their preference for the present. As a result, the structure will shrink horizontally and elongate vertically. More specifically:

- Expenditure decreases in the lower stages as consumer spending declines (shrinkage downward).
- Investment spending increases in the upper stages, leading to growth in those areas (enlargement upward).
- New stages emerge at the top of the structure (extension).

Capital accumulation is easily visualized using this type of diagram, as it represents a deformation of the triangle illustrating the structure. In Hayek's simple example, interest payments are ignored: nominal consumption falls from 40 to 30 (net saving = 10), investment spending correspondingly rises from 80 to 90, and investment per stage decreases linearly. As a result of the net saving of 10, the initial five-stage structure shifts to a more capital-intensive seven-stage structure (see Fig. 5.7). Once production factors are reallocated to higher stages, the lengthened structure allows for greater final production, as the production "detour" has increased (see Sect. 5.1.8). Consequently, capital accumulation, after a temporary fall in the production of consumer goods per period (sacrifice of saving), leads to an increase in this amount.

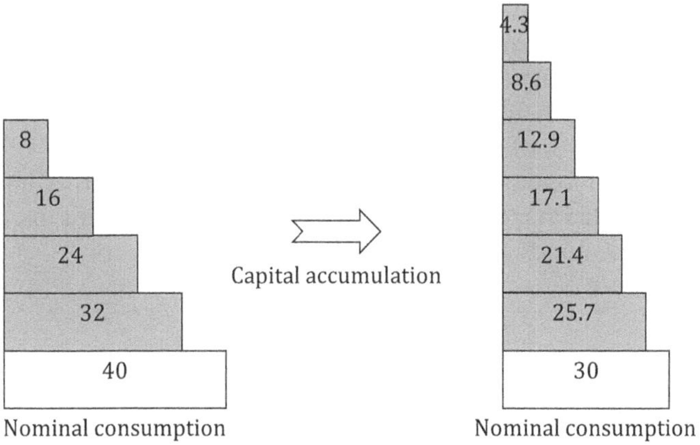

Fig. 5.7 Hayek's illustration of capital accumulation (1931, p. 44 and p. 52)

5.2.8 *Critique of the "Paradox of Saving"*

The scenario we have just explored—where consumption spending declines in favor of savings and investment—has often been cited, even today, as a potential cause of economic crises. According to the *theory of underconsumption*, depressions and mass unemployment arise from a reduction in consumption. In essence, this theory posits that insufficient consumption leads to unprofitable production. Specifically, if households cut back on their consumption expenditures, the prices of consumer goods tend to fall. Conversely, if households simultaneously increase their investment spending, the prices of factors of production tend to rise. As a result, the selling prices of final goods may become inadequate to cover their production costs, leading companies to incur losses, reduce production, and lay off workers—ultimately resulting in mass unemployment and recession. This seems to give rise to a "paradox of saving": an individual who saves becomes wealthier, but if many individuals attempt to save simultaneously, they will impoverish society by triggering a crisis of underconsumption.

Hayek (1939 [1929], p. 224) argues that this reasoning is flawed because it fails to account for the existence of the production structure, which reflects the fact that production occurs in successive stages. It is incorrect to compare the average price movements of consumer goods and factors of production, as these prices vary differently across different stages. Hayek's critique of this "paradox" is rooted in an analysis of how the price system functions during the capital accumulation phase.

In the lower stages, closer to consumption, a decline in demand for consumer goods results in lower prices. This price drop is transmitted to the factors of production in the stages just above, leading to a decrease in their prices as well. Consequently, profitability decreases in the lower stages, particularly the closer they are to final consumption (as the impact of reduced consumer spending is more pronounced at these stages).

The increase in savings and investment "feeds" the higher stages, generating profits there. As capital is reallocated to these upper stages, it contributes to increased demand, thereby raising the selling prices of factors of production and enhancing profits—particularly in stages closer to the top of the structure. As a result, convertible factors of production tend to be shifted from the bottom to the top of the structure, increasing the production "detour" and ultimately enhancing the productivity of the economic system.

As Fig. 5.8 illustrates, the initial shift in intertemporal preferences—marked by a decrease in present consumption and an increase in savings and investment—leads to reduced profitability in the lower stages while increasing it in the higher stages. This reallocation of factors from the bottom to the top of the structure restores equilibrium by lowering prices in

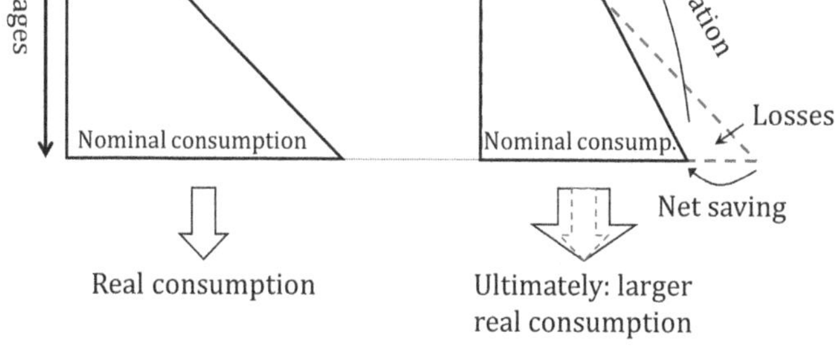

Fig. 5.8 A representation of the capital accumulation process

the higher stages and raising them in the lower stages, thereby equalizing the rates of return across the structure. This mechanism of the price system mirrors the processes described earlier (see Sects. 3.2.11 and 3.2.13): a shock causes rates of return to diverge across various sectors of the economic system, prompting entrepreneurs to reallocate factors from low- to high-profitability sectors. This reorganization of production ultimately brings rates of return back into alignment. Thus, the so-called paradox of saving disappears: a decline in consumption combined with an increase in savings and investment does not precipitate a crisis of global overproduction or impoverish society; rather, it enriches society by lengthening the production process.

Here are, in summary, the not-at-all paradoxical effects of a capital accumulation resulting from a net saving: temporary losses in the lower stages, temporary profits in the higher stages, reallocation of factors toward the top of the structure, an overall lengthening of the production process, and, ultimately, increased production once the new, longer structure is fully operational.

5.2.9 *The Reappraisal of Savings and Investment*

The Austrian theory of the structure of production significantly reevaluates the role of savings and investment in comparison to Keynesian macroeconomic theory.

From a static perspective, the conventional measure of GDP for a given year substantially underrepresents the significance and impact of investment on the functioning of the economic system. According to Skousen's estimate for the United States in 1982, total product (GNO: gross national output) is twice the size of GNP (gross national product), with consumption constituting only 34% of total economic activity as measured by GNO, while it represents 65% of GNP. In other words, relative to standard indicators, the importance of investment is effectively doubled, whereas the significance of consumption is halved.

From a dynamic perspective, the resolution of the so-called paradox of saving clarifies the Austrian critique of the Keynesian view that an increase in savings and investment can act as a harmful "leakage" in the economic system. For Austrians, an increase in savings does not lead to paradoxical effects; instead, it facilitates the production of greater wealth and enhances living standards—at the price of a temporary sacrifice. Skousen (1990, p. 244) illustrates the strong correlation between savings rates and economic growth, attributing this relationship as one of the factors behind the remarkable growth observed in the "Asian Tigers" during the latter half of the twentieth century.

References

Clark, J. B. (1899). *The Distribution of Wealth. A Theory of Wages, Interest, and Profits*. Macmillan.

Fetter, F. (1915). *Economic Principles*. Century.

Garrison, R. W. (2001). *Time and Money. The Macroeconomics of the Capital Structure*. Routledge.

Hayek, F. A. (1931). *Prices and Production*. George Routledge and Sons.

Hayek, F. A. (1936). The Mythology of Capital. *Quarterly Journal of Economics, 50*(2), 199–228.

Hayek, F. A. (1939 [1929]). The "Paradox" of Saving. In F. A. Hayek (Ed.), *Profits, Interest and Investment, and Other Essays on the Theory of Industrial Fluctuations* (pp. 199–263). George Routledge & Sons.

Hayek, F. A. (1941). *The Pure Theory of Capital*. The University of Chicago Press.

Huerta de Soto, J. (2006 [1998]). *Money, Bank Credit, and Economic Cycles*. Ludwig von Mises Institute.

Jevons, W. S. (1965 [1871]). *The Theory of Political Economy*. Augustus M. Kelley.

Knight, F. H. (1934). Capital, Time, and the Interest Rate. *Economica, 1*(3), 257–286.

Menger, C. (1976 [1871]). *Principles of Economics*. New York University Press.

Mill, J. S. (1987 [1848]). *Principles of Political Economy with Some of their Applications to Social Philosophy*. Augustus M. Kelley.

Reisman, G. (1996). *Capitalism. A Treatise on Economics*. Jameson Books.

Rothbard, M. N. (1962). *Man, Economy, and State. A Treatise on Economic Principles*. D. Van Nostrand.

Skousen, M. (1990). *The Structure of Production*. New York University Press.

von Böhm-Bawerk, E. (1959 [1889]). *Positive Theory of Capital*. Libertarian Press.

von Mises, L. (1981 [1922]). *Socialism. An Economic and Sociological Analysis*. LibertyClassics.

von Mises, L. (1998 [1949]). *Human Action. A Treatise on Economics*. Ludwig von Mises Institute.

Wicksell, K. (1954 [1893]). *Value, Capital and Rent*. George Allen and Unwin.

CHAPTER 6

Capital and Interest

Abstract This chapter highlights key debates within the Austrian School itself, such as the "real" versus "nominal" conceptions of capital and competing explanations for interest, including productivity, time preference, and loanable funds theories. It then critiques Classical and socialist perspectives on the topic interest, for instance the abstinence and exploitation theories, while emphasizing the importance of intertemporal valuation.

Keywords Capital • Interest rate • Time preference • Productivity

Although Menger laid the groundwork with his theories on capital and interest, it was Böhm-Bawerk's major treatise (1959a [1884], 1959b [1889]) that became the foundation for more extensive discussions on these topics within the Austrian School. Some of Böhm-Bawerk's ideas were quickly challenged by Fetter (1900, 1902). A significant divide then arose: on one side were Böhm-Bawerk, Wicksell, and Hayek, who supported a real conception of capital and a productivity theory of interest; on the other were Fetter, Mises, and Rothbard, who advocated for a nominal definition of capital and a subjectivist theory of interest rooted in time preference. These differences run deep, particularly in their explanations

R. Fillieule, *The Austrian School of Economics*, Palgrave Studies in Austrian Economics,
https://doi.org/10.1007/978-3-031-83414-1_6

of interest, with at least five distinct theories being defended by Austrian economists: a use theory, a productivity theory, a time preference theory, a time-market theory, and the loanable funds markets theory.

6.1 Factors of Production and Capital

6.1.1 From Classical Distribution Theory to the Imputation Principle

Ricardo (1951 [1817]) developed the Classical theory of distribution, distinguishing three main types of income—rent, wages, and profit—corresponding to the three factors of production: land, labor, and capital. Each income type is explained by a specific theory: rent theory for income from land, the subsistence theory for labor income, and the residual income theory for profit (what Ricardo refers to as "profit" is actually the interest on invested capital, representing what remains for the capitalist after production costs are covered).

Menger's imputation theory (see Sect. 2.3.1) fundamentally challenges the Ricardian framework. He argues that land and labor, as higher-order goods, have subjective value and prices *determined by the same principles*: their value to an individual depends on the needs they help satisfy, and their price is set by the interaction of supply and demand, driven by these subjective evaluations. Ricardo and his followers proposed a general price theory based on labor costs (where the price of reproducible goods is proportional to the labor needed to produce them) and specific theories for non-produced factors (land and labor). In contrast, Menger unified *all types of goods* under a single theory of value and price. Regarding profit (or interest income), he attributes it to the use of capital, though the details of this belong to the theory of interest, which will be discussed later.

Mises (1981 [1922], p. 131) notes that the term "distribution," while widely used, is merely a metaphor that does not accurately reflect how a market economy operates. In a market economy, goods are not first produced and then distributed; the production process is inseparable from the market exchanges that determine income. The issue of distribution in its literal sense only arises in interventionist systems where taxes are collected and redistributed. Therefore, in a market economy, it is more appropriate to speak of a theory of higher-order goods prices.

6.1.2 The "Real" Conception of Capital

Austrian economists have adopted two contrasting views of capital: one identifying it with *material goods* (the "real" conception) and the other with *monetary value* (the "nominal" conception). Böhm-Bawerk supports the "real" view, defining capital as all produced factors of production (1959b [1889], p. 14). Capital is thus distinct from land (which is not produced, such as natural resources), labor (immaterial services), and consumer goods (which are the final goal of production, not a means of production). In this sense, any society beyond the most basic level of subsistence possesses capital, even if only in the form of rudimentary tools.

This materialist definition, as it might be called, was adopted with variations by Wicksell and Hayek. Wicksell (1954 [1893], p. 105) classifies material production factors based on their durability. The most durable factors, even if produced, are categorized under "land" and are called "rent goods," while factors consumed quickly during production are classified as "capital goods." Hayek (1941, p. 53) builds on this by substituting "durability" with "permanence." For him, non-permanent factors that are used up in the production process are part of capital, while permanent (non-consumable) factors are not. The examples he offers of permanent factors are water power and the productive power of the soil. Like Wicksell, Hayek rejects the distinction between original and produced factors, seeing it as a vestige of the labor theory of value. He argues that capital, like any economic category, should focus on the future, not the past. Whether a factor results from a production process is a historical question, not an economic one.

These three proponents of the "real" conception of capital align with the productivity theory of interest, while those who advocate for the "nominal" conception support the subjectivist theory, which explains interest through time preference.

Can We Distinguish Between "Land" and "Capital"?

Böhm-Bawerk maintains the classical distinction between "land" (an unproduced material factor of production) and "capital" (a produced material factor of production). Similarly, as we have seen, Wicksell and Hayek differentiate between these based on the durability or permanence of material factors, excluding highly durable or permanent goods from capital, regardless of whether they were previously produced.

Fetter (1900), however, strongly challenges this traditional distinction, arguing that *all* material factors of production should be considered part of capital. He specifically refutes Böhm-Bawerk's arguments for separating land from capital based on the previous application of labor. For example, removing rocks from an agricultural field is a permanent improvement, but does this make the improved field capital (as the result of labor) or land (an immovable gift of nature that cannot be increased)? Fetter likely would have criticized Wicksell and Hayek's distinction as well, arguing that durability is too vague (at what point in time does a capital good become a rent good, i.e., "land"?). The core reason Fetter rejects the land versus capital distinction is that he advocates a nominal, not a real, conception of capital.

Rothbard (1962) disagrees with Fetter's view, arguing that there is a key criterion for distinguishing between land and capital: *reproducibility*. Land is not reproducible, and therefore the rent it generates is net income. In contrast, capital goods are reproducible, and they generate a gross income, from which production costs must be deducted to determine net income. In equilibrium, this net income equals the interest earned.

6.1.3 The "Nominal" Conception of Capital

In the Austrian tradition, the nominal conception of capital can be traced back to Menger. While Menger embraces the "real" conception in his main treatise, in a later work on the theory of capital (Menger, 1888), he defines capital as the monetary value of property, aligning with how the term is used in the business world. Influenced by Clark and Fisher, Fetter (1900) also adopts this nominal conception, demonstrating that it transcends traditional distinctions such as social versus private capital, land versus capital, and even factors of production versus consumer goods (since a consumer good, if it can be sold or resold, possesses capital value).

Material objects can be classified differently depending on the perspective:

1. From the perspective of satisfying needs, they are *goods*.
2. From a legal standpoint (ownership rights), they are *property*.
3. From the standpoint of their value (market price), they are *capital*.

Fetter (1977, p. 149) expands this notion of capital beyond material goods, including assets like credits, customer bases, franchises, and patents. Mises (1981 [1922], p. 106) follows Menger by defining capital as a concept tied to economic calculation and accounting. He highlights that the concept of capital, along with the related concept of *income*, is crucial in a market economy, enabling individuals to assess how much of their resources can be consumed in the present without compromising future needs (i.e., capital maintenance). If consumption exceeds income, capital is depleted; if consumption is less than income, capital is saved and accumulated. In a complex economic system, monetary calculation is essential, as the physical description of various heterogeneous production factors provides no insight into their ability to meet human needs. Mises (1998 [1949], p. 262) defines capital as "the sum of the money equivalent of all assets minus the sum of the money equivalent of all liabilities," with these assets comprising claims and material goods of all kinds (land, buildings, tools, consumer goods, money, etc.).

6.1.4 Generalizing the Notion of Rent

Fetter expanded the concept of capital to include all material factors of production and similarly generalized the notion of rent. Traditionally, rent refers to income derived from land, but Fetter argues that it is "impossible" to draw a clear distinction between land and capital goods in practice (1901, p. 320). Therefore, he asserts that "rent" should be understood as the *income earned per unit of time* from *all* material factors of production, not just those related to land.

Furthermore, the classical Ricardian concept of rent requires revision. Ricardo viewed rent as residual income, meaning it was generated by the productive efficiency of land but not considered part of production costs. Fetter (1901) argues that both Ricardo and Marshall, who adopted Ricardo's view, were mistaken. The classical belief that rent is not a production cost arose from the idea that land is a "free" gift of nature, with no "real cost" of production, since no labor or sacrifice was required to obtain it. This lack of real cost was incorrectly equated with a zero monetary cost. For Fetter, this reasoning is flawed: rent is indeed a monetary production cost that must be accounted for by the producer, whether landowner or tenant, when calculating net income from their activities.

While Fetter does not explicitly refer to Menger in this context, his reasoning applies the imputation principle: real costs do not affect the value or price of goods. The fact that "land" factors have zero real cost does not give them any special status in terms of value or price compared to other factors.

Mises (1998 [1949], p. 668) acknowledges the classical theory of rent, noting that it anticipated marginalism, and regrets that Ricardo did not realize his theory offered a general solution to the problem of determining the prices of all factors, including labor.

6.1.5 *Rent and Capitalization*

If factors of production provide rent to their owners (and cost that rent to those who purchase them), what, then, is the nature of interest income? According to Fetter, rent and interest should not be seen as distinct incomes tied to different types of production factors. Instead, they represent different perspectives on the income generated by goods:

- *Rent* is the income derived from goods viewed in terms of their wealth aspect.
- *Interest* is the income from goods considered as (nominal) capital.

To be more precise, rent reflects the price of goods for the current unit of time, while interest represents a form of capitalization income, arising from the difference between the present and future prices of those goods.

Fetter's argument can be illustrated with an example. Imagine a producer wanting to purchase a factor F now (at time t_0) that will generate an income R in 1 year (at time t_1). How much would the producer be willing to pay at t_0 to acquire this factor? The producer would not pay R, because by investing that amount elsewhere at the current annual interest rate i, they would receive $R(1 + i)$ in t_1, which is more than R. Instead, they would pay the present value of F, which is the capitalized value, $R \div (1 + i)$. If they manage to buy it for less, they would gain entrepreneurial profit; if they pay more, they would incur a loss.

Thus, at t_1, the producer will earn:

- Rent (R), which is the *synchronous* income corresponding to the monetary productivity of factor F at time t_1.
- Interest, calculated as R—$[R \div (1 + i)]$, which is the *diachronic* income arising from the difference between the income R generated from the use or sale of F at t_1 and its purchase price $R \div (1 + i)$ at t_0.

This concept can be generalized to durable goods used over multiple periods. For instance, consider a durable good that generates \$5000 after

1 year, another $5000 after 2 years, and continues for 4 years. Assuming an interest rate of 3%, the present (capitalized) value of the good would be calculated accordingly.

$$\frac{5000}{1+0.03}+\frac{5000}{(1+0.03)^2}+\frac{5000}{(1+0.03)^3}+\frac{5000}{(1+0.03)^4}$$

It is as if the producer had purchased a first unit of the factor for $5000 ÷ (1 + 0.03), which would yield $5000 after 1 year (reflecting an interest rate of 3%). A second unit of the factor would be purchased for $5000 ÷ (1 + 0.03)², yielding $5000 after 2 years, again with a 3% annual interest rate, and so on. In this way, the producer secures an annual rent of $5000 while earning a 3% interest rate on each unit of the factor.

In the nominal conception of capital, material production factors generate both rent and interest, depending on the time perspective from which the income is viewed (see Fig. 6.1).

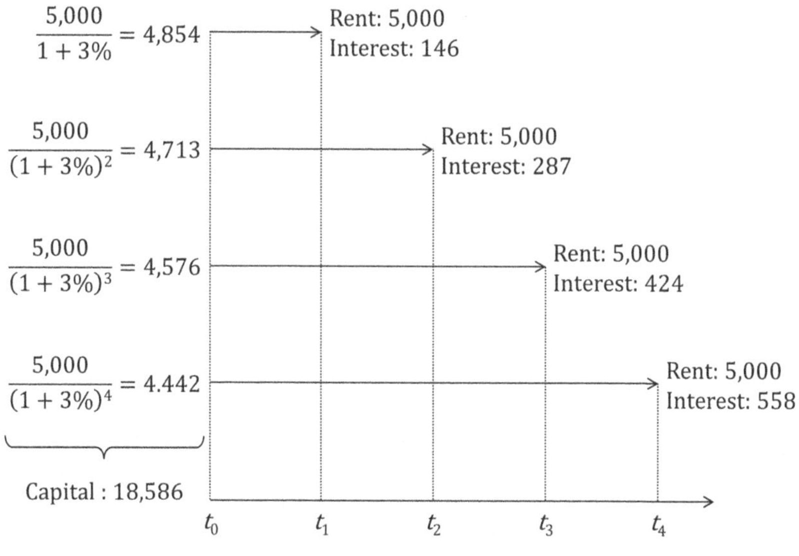

Fig. 6.1 Rent and interest on a capital investment of $18,585: the asset will generate $5000 in annual rental income and earn 3% annual interest for 4 years

This reasoning assumes the existence of an interest rate. However, Fetter's "capitalization theory" goes further, as it explains the very existence of interest based on the preference for present consumption. The phenomenon of capitalization (discounting future goods) precedes and explains the formation of the interest rate itself (see Sect. 6.2.6).

6.1.6 Austrian Income Theory: Rent, Interest, Profit, and Loss

For Fetter, followed by Mises and Rothbard, all factors of production generate both rent (synchronous income) and interest (diachronic income). This applies equally to original and produced factors, as well as to material goods and immaterial services. Rent reflects the productivity of a factor—its ability to satisfy needs—when assessed from a synchronous perspective. Interest, on the other hand, represents the price difference between present and future goods (see Sect. 6.2.6).

A broader distinction exists between *static incomes* (rent and interest), which persist in equilibrium, and *dynamic incomes* (entrepreneurial profits and losses), which only arise in disequilibrium. Key theoretical distinctions regarding factors of production include:

- *Higher-order* versus *lower-order factors*: Higher-order factors derive their value and price from lower-order goods (imputation principle).
- *Convertible* versus *specific factors*: The prices of convertible factors are imputed from their marginal product, while the price of specific original factors is a residual, calculated as the remainder after subtracting other factor prices from the process' total income (Rothbard, 1962).
- *Original* versus *produced factors*: Original factors provide a net income, whereas the gross income from produced factors is entirely consumed by production costs and interest on the capital invested to produce them.

The Austrian theory of distribution is no longer about the distribution of total income among social classes (workers, landowners, capitalists). Instead, it is a *functional distribution* theory, where individuals can simultaneously be workers, capitalists, landowners, and entrepreneurs, receiving income from various activities (Clark, 1899).

6.1.7 *Capitalism*

Böhm-Bawerk, who defines capital as the produced factors of production (capital goods), considers an economy "capitalist" as soon as it uses tools and intermediate goods. For Mises, however, who adopts the nominal conception of capital, the notion of "capitalism" is quite different. Capital, understood as the monetary equivalent of assets, relies on the existence of institutions like private property, exchange, and money. Thus, capitalism is not a general category of all human societies but specifically one within a market economy. The term "capitalism" is fitting to describe a system where monetary capital calculation serves as the primary tool for productive rationality.

6.2 Theories of Interest

6.2.1 *The Theoretical Problem of Interest*

Interest is the income derived from capital, and as Böhm-Bawerk (1959a [1884], p. 1) points out, it has several notable features:

- It is earned effortlessly by the capitalist.
- It does not depend on the specific material form of the capital goods in which the capital is invested.
- It tends to be proportional to the capital invested, typically represented as a uniform percentage known as the interest rate.
- In principle, it can be earned indefinitely.

A theory of interest must explain the origin of this unique flow of wealth, which is acquired effortlessly and continuously. Böhm-Bawerk makes an important distinction between the *theoretical* problem of interest—which seeks to identify the causes of interest—and the *moral* problem of interest, which questions whether this income is just and proper. To determine the moral justification of interest, one must first understand its source.

6.2.2 *Originary Interest and Contractual Interest*

Interest income can take two forms that Böhm-Bawerk calls "originary" interest and "contractual" interest. Producers generally sell their products for more than the cost of production, and the difference between the selling price and the production cost constitutes originary interest (as distinct from entrepreneurial profit, a point that will be clarified later).

Interest income can also be contractual, where the interest is fixed by a loan agreement. However, originary interest is the more fundamental form of interest. Without originary interest, capitalists would not be able to earn contractual interest by lending money to companies. In other words, the ability of capitalists to receive contractual interest from loans is based on the fact that production tends to generate originary interest. As Fetter (1914, p. 234) explains, originary interest holds both logical and historical precedence over contractual interest.

6.2.3 *Originary Interest and Entrepreneurial Profit*

The difference between the selling price of products and the cost of production factors is not a uniform amount. It consists of two components: interest and entrepreneurial profit. Böhm-Bawerk acknowledges that, in practice, distinguishing between the two can be challenging. He suggests using the typical interest rate in the industry as a guide. For instance, if a company has invested $100,000 and earns a surplus of $9000 in a given year, with a prevailing interest rate of 5%, the interest income would be $5000, and the entrepreneurial profit would amount to $4000.

Mises (1998 [1949], p. 533) points out that the issue is more complex because all market interest rates include an element of uncertainty due to the unpredictability of the future. As a result, no market data can perfectly isolate the originary interest rate from entrepreneurial profit.

Böhm-Bawerk attributes profit to the "personal effort" of the entrepreneur—whether through oversight, strategic decision-making, or simply the will to invest in one company over another. He regards profit as a form of remuneration for labor. Mises (1998 [1949], p. 532) offers a more detailed breakdown, distinguishing between originary interest, the managerial wage (payment for labor), and entrepreneurial profit or loss (stemming from future uncertainty). Additionally, monetary factors, such as changes in the value of money, may affect these calculations (see Sect. 7.2.15).

6.2.4 *Interest as a Phenomenon of Intertemporal Valuation (Böhm-Bawerk)*

Böhm-Bawerk (1959b [1889], p. 259) bases his theory of interest on the idea that present goods are generally more valuable than future goods (see

Sect. 2.2.12). This principle helps explain the three main forms in which interest manifests.

Interest on Loans (Contractual Interest): A money loan involves an exchange where individual *A* gives up a present good (a sum of money) and individual *B* promises to repay with a future good (a future sum of money). Since a sum of money available in the future is worth less than the same amount in the present, the lender will demand a higher sum in repayment. The borrower must agree to these terms or risk not securing the loan (unless, perhaps, they find a benefactor willing to help, like a family member). The additional amount paid back to the lender represents the interest.

Interest on Investment (Originary Interest): For Böhm-Bawerk, factors of production are considered "future goods" because it takes time for the production process to transform them into consumer goods that can satisfy needs. Therefore, factors of production are valued less than the final goods they help produce. For example, the value of factors used today to produce two tons of wheat in a year is less than the value of two tons of wheat available today. More broadly, since production factors are future goods, their price is discounted compared to present goods, and this price difference constitutes interest.

Interest on Durable Goods: A durable good provides services over multiple periods. The services rendered in the future are considered future goods, and thus, they are worth less when valued today. If a durable good is expected to generate \$1000 per year for 3 years, its "capital value" (the sum of all its services) will be less than \$3000 because future services are discounted. For instance, with a 5% annual discount rate, the first year's service is today worth \$1000 ÷ (1 + 5%) = \$952, the second year's is worth \$1000 ÷ $(1 + 5\%)^2$ = \$907, and the third year's \$1000 ÷ $(1 + 5\%)^3$ = \$864. The total capital value would thus be \$952 + \$907 + \$864 = \$2723. This process of discounting also explains why land, which provides services indefinitely, still has a finite price (Böhm-Bawerk, 1959a [1889], p. 334). Indeed, the infinite sum of a rent *R* discounted at the interest rate *i* is a finite number, as seen in the perpetuity formula:

$$\frac{R}{1+i}+\frac{R}{(1+i)^2}+\frac{R}{(1+i)^3}+\frac{R}{(1+i)^4}+\cdots=\frac{R}{i}$$

6.2.5 *The Capital Productivity Theory (Böhm-Bawerk, Wicksell, Hayek)*

To address how the originary interest rate is determined, Böhm-Bawerk developed a theory based on the productivity of capital. In the Austrian framework, this productivity is linked to the length of the production period (see Sect. 5.1.8). His theory is technical, but a brief summary can be given, noting that Wicksell (1954 [1893]) provides an elegant graphical illustration, later enhanced by Dorfman (1959).

Böhm-Bawerk (1959b [1889]) examines an economic system where the production function (as shown in Fig. 4.1) is fixed. He assumes there is only one type of labor and that the monthly wage is also fixed. He demonstrates that capitalists can maximize the interest rate by selecting an optimal total production period. For each wage level (w), there is an "optimal" production length $l^*(w)$ that maximizes the interest rate, and this optimal length increases as wages rise.

Böhm-Bawerk also considers the capital constraint—how much total capital is available to fund the production structure. If the available capital is insufficient to support a production length of l^*, competition among workers will drive wages down, shortening the production structure until an equilibrium wage (w_e), compatible with the available capital, is reached. Conversely, if there is excess capital, competition among capitalists for workers will raise the wage to its equilibrium level w_e, lengthening the production period to $l^*(w_e)$. Thus, the interest rate is determined by capitalists' choices, based on the overall production function and the available capital.

Hayek (1941) also supports the productivity view that interest reflects the marginal productivity of capital—that is, the additional output gained per period by adding one stage to the structure. However, he rejects Böhm-Bawerk's simplifying assumptions of an average production period (l) and a fixed quantity of capital (K). He also factors in agents' intertemporal preferences as a secondary consideration in determining the interest rate (see Fillieule, 2017 and 2022, for an in-depth analysis of Hayek's theory).

6.2.6 *The Time-Preference or Capitalization Theory (Fetter, Mises)*

Fetter and Mises argue that Böhm-Bawerk effectively refuted productivity theories in his critique of Classical interest theories (see Sect. 6.2.9). They contend that he contradicted himself and erred by developing a productivity theory. They assert that originary interest cannot be explained by analyzing increases in the quantities or values produced. If factors of production lead to the creation of more valuable goods, that value will be imputed to the factors themselves, leaving the difference between price and cost unexplained.

According to Fetter and Mises, originary interest arises from and is an aggregate outcome of individuals' intertemporal choices. All goods are dated, meaning they are available at specific points in time. Decisions regarding supply and demand inherently possess a temporal aspect since they involve these dated goods. Given their preference for the present, individuals tend to favor present goods, which results in a premium for them and, conversely, a discount for future goods.

These price differentials tend to converge percentage-wise, leading to a generally uniform interest rate. Entrepreneurs, seeking the highest possible percentage differential, will bid up the prices of factors and increase production whenever the market returns exceed the average. This process raises unit costs and lowers selling prices, thereby narrowing the percentage gap between price and cost until it returns to the average. Similarly, if the percentage gap falls below the average, it will tend to rise back toward it (see Sect. 3.2.11). Therefore, the phenomenon of originary interest permeates the market economy and is inextricably linked to the prices of goods available at different moments in time.

If the services of future goods are discounted—such as when a good expected to yield $1000 in a year is purchased today for $950—it is not due to the existence of an interest rate. Rather, it is because future services are discounted in value that an interest rate appears. This foundation is what Fetter (1914, p. 230) refers to as "capitalization theory." In this view, capitalization—essentially the discounting of the value and price of future goods—logically and historically precedes the phenomenon of the interest rate and provides its explanation.

Variations in originary interest are explained within this framework by changes in preferences for the present. If the preference for the present declines—meaning that individuals now place a higher value on future consumption than on present consumption—then the value and price of future goods will rise, while those of present goods will fall. This reduction in the price gap constitutes a decrease in the rate of originary interest. Conversely, if the preference for the present increases, the demand for present goods rises while the demand for future goods decreases. This dynamic increases the gap between the prices of present and future goods, leading to a rise in the originary interest rate. Mises (1998 [1949], p. 524) illustrates this concept with the example of a population that believes the end of the world is imminent: their preference for the present will surge, leading to a high premium for present goods (and a large discount for future goods), thereby causing a sharp increase in originary interest.

6.2.7 *The Time-Market Theory (Rothbard)*

Böhm-Bawerk (1959b [1889], p. 287) briefly outlines a theory of exchange, which Rothbard (1962, p. 319) elaborates on in detail. According to Rothbard, the interest rate is established in the market for the exchange of present and future goods, a market he refers to as the "time market." This market encompasses not only consumer loans but also all production processes. In fact, purchasing factors of production involves sacrificing a present good (money, which Rothbard considers the quintessential present good) in exchange for a future good (the monetary income earned at the end of production). Within this framework, Rothbard examines the determination of the "pure" interest rate, meaning the rate that exists in the absence of uncertainty.

Each actor in the market is characterized by an intertemporal preference profile, which reflects a stronger or weaker preference for the present, as well as the wealth they currently possess and their expectations for future wealth. For various potential interest rates between the present and future periods (e.g., 1%, 2%, 3%), each actor decides whether to borrow—if the rate is low enough—or to lend—if the rate offers sufficient returns.

- The sum of the portions of the individual curves corresponding to potential loans or investments forms the supply curve for present goods (in exchange for future goods received as repayment in the subsequent period). This curve is upward-sloping: as the interest rate increases, the quantity of present money offered for loans increases because the potential remuneration becomes more attractive.
- Conversely, the sum of the individual curves related to borrowing or receiving invested money constitutes the demand curve for present goods (in exchange for future goods). This curve is downward-sloping: as the interest rate rises, the cost of repayment becomes higher, leading to a decrease in the quantity of money borrowed.

By comparing these two curves, we can identify an equilibrium interest rate at which the quantity of present money spent on production equals the quantity borrowed or received (see Fig. 6.2). If the interest rate

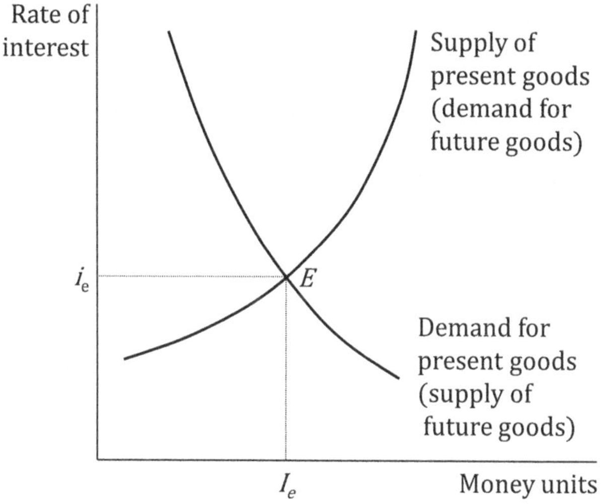

Fig. 6.2 Determining the equilibrium pure interest rate (Rothbard, 1962, p. 332)

exceeds this equilibrium rate, not all suppliers of present money will find borrowers and they will have to lower their "price," that is, their interest rate, to attract buyers. Conversely, if the rate is below the equilibrium, it will tend to rise. The pure interest rate is thus determined in a manner similar to the price in an auction market.

6.2.8 *The Loanable Funds Theory*

From the outset of his treatise, Böhm-Bawerk clearly identifies the primary objective of the theory of interest: to explain the phenomenon of originary interest. Like him, many members of the Austrian School contend that the existence of originary interest logically precedes that of contractual interest (Fetter, 1927, p. 275; Mises, 1998 [1949], p. 524; Hayek, 1941, p. 266; Rothbard, 1962, p. 364). In their view, the contractual interest that arises in the market for loanable funds is a secondary and derivative phenomenon that cannot fundamentally explain interest. However, more recent scholars from the Austrian School, such as Skousen (1990), Horwitz (2000), and Garrison (2001), have adopted the theory of the market for loanable funds to elucidate the level of interest rates.

This theory applies the auction model, similar to Rothbard's exchange theory, but focuses specifically on the market for loanable funds (see Fig. 6.3). Monetary savings, which increase as the interest rate rises, represent the supply of funds. Entrepreneurs are willing to borrow larger amounts of money when interest rates are lower, reflecting the demand for funds, which decreases as the interest rate increases. The interest rate tends to settle at the equilibrium level that balances the quantity of funds lent with the quantity borrowed.

If the interest rate is above this equilibrium level, the supply of funds exceeds demand, leading savers to compete to invest their funds. As a result, they have to lower their demands to avoid missing out on profitable exchange opportunities, causing the rate to decline toward equilibrium. Conversely, if the rate is below equilibrium, it will tend to rise. Importantly, this theory of loanable funds is not uniquely "Austrian"; it is also a standard model presented in introductory textbooks such as Mankiw (2010).

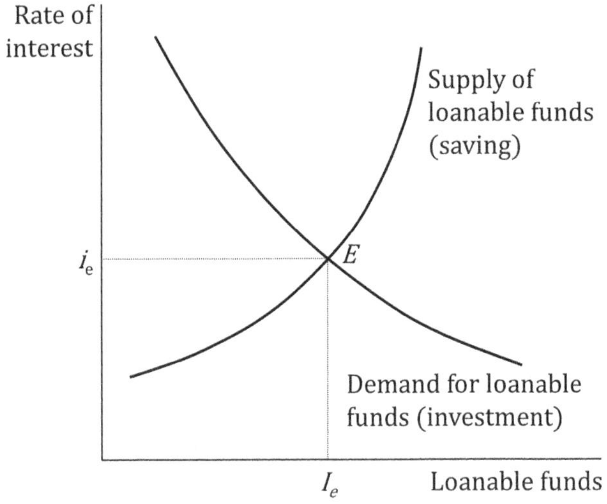

Fig. 6.3 The loanable funds market (after Skousen, 1990, p. 204)

6.2.9 *Critique of Classical Theories of Interest: Productivity, Abstinence, Remuneration*

During the "classical" period, which spanned from the publication of Adam Smith's treatise in 1776 (1976 [1776]) to the Neoclassical revolution of the 1870s, several significant theories of interest were developed. These theories were subjected to rigorous critical analysis by Böhm-Bawerk (1959a [1884]).

The Productivity Theory (Say, Lauderdale, Malthus, Thünen, etc.). This theory holds that "capital"—including tools, machines, and similar assets—is "productive" because it enables the production of goods in larger quantities or of higher quality. These more plentiful or superior goods can then command a higher revenue, which is argued to constitute interest. However, this theory is easily challenged within the Austrian framework. Since the value of products is imputed to their factors, a factor that contributes to a more valuable product will itself become more expensive. Therefore, it is impossible to explain interest by the higher income received thanks to the use in production of more numerous or advanced capital goods, as these capital goods will also carry higher prices. The core issue in explaining interest is to understand why the price gap between products and their factors persists, rather than disappearing entirely due to imputation. The productivity theory overlooks this imputation process and thus fails both to address this problem and to provide a solution.

The Abstinence Theory (Senior, Bastiat, Cairnes). This theory posits that interest is the reward the capitalist receives for abstaining from present consumption, which is essentially the sacrifice made through savings and investment. According to Senior (1836), the capitalist's abstinence from consumption constitutes a cost that must be included in the selling price. This theory characterizes interest as a form of "abstinence wage," which is added to workers' wages to determine the selling price. Menger (1976 [1871], p. 156) provides a concise critique of this theory, arguing that production costs—whether they stem from labor or abstinence—can *never* explain why goods possess value. Therefore, they cannot account for interest. Böhm-Bawerk identifies an additional flaw in Senior's reasoning. For instance, a capitalist might pay $100 today for wages that will yield returns in a year. According to Senior, this capitalist experiences two sacrifices: one in wages ($100) and another in abstinence (waiting a year for income from the investment). However, Böhm-Bawerk contends that, in reality, the capitalist has made *only one* sacrifice, the $100, and none other. Thus, even if one were to accept a "classical" explanation of interest based on production costs, Senior's theory of abstinence remains unsatisfactory.

The Remuneration Theory (Courcelle-Seneuil and the "socialists of the chair"). In this theory, interest is simply seen as compensation for the labor services provided by the capitalist. This labor might include efforts to accumulate and preserve savings—an undertaking requiring both will and intelligence—thus earning a wage in the form of interest. However, this theory faces a critical inconsistency: large capital yields higher interest income while small capital yields lower interest income. If we assume that capitalists exert effort, that effort does not inherently increase with the size of the capital. Consequently, the income disparity between large and small capital remains unexplained by the theory of remuneration. Böhm-Bawerk succinctly critiques this perspective by asserting that interest is not derived from labor but rather from property.

6.2.10 Critique of the Exploitation Theory

Developed by socialists such as Rodbertus, Proudhon, Lassalle, Marx, etc., this theory posits that only labor produces wealth. Consequently, interest is viewed as wealth generated by workers but extorted from them by capitalists who take advantage of their control over privately owned capital. In Rodbertus' version, workers receive only their "reproduction" wage—the minimum subsistence wage—while the surplus is confiscated as interest. Menger (1976 [1871], p. 168) already offered a brief critique of a foundational aspect of this theory, stating that wealth is not solely the product of labor. Böhm-Bawerk builds upon this criticism and presents several additional arguments, the most compelling of which is as follows.

Consider a production process that pays only labor (with capital goods and land assumed to be free). Suppose this process lasts a year and results in a product sold for $10,500. If labor is compensated based on the full value of its output, then it is valued at $10,500. However, the crucial question remains: *when* is this value determined? Proponents of the exploitation theory miss this essential point. If a capitalist finances this process, how much will he be willing to pay? Assuming an annual interest rate of 5%, the capitalist will only proceed with financing if the worker agrees to be paid $10,000 or less. Should the worker require more than $10,000, the capitalist would incur a loss, as he would receive only $10,500 a year later, yielding a lower interest return than the current 5% obtained anywhere else.

This situation means that the labor value paid at the start of the process is only $10,000, while if it were compensated at the end, it would amount to $10,500. Therefore, a worker who receives $10,000 *at the beginning* of the process effectively captures the *full* value of his labor; if he were to invest that sum for a year at a 5% interest rate, he would indeed receive the $10,500 that reflects the product's selling price when it becomes available.

Even in a scenario utilizing only labor, there is *no incompatibility* between the capitalist earning interest income (in this case, $500 *at the end* of the process) and the worker receiving the full value of his labor (here, $10,000 *at the start*). Should the capitalist pay the worker less than $10,000, he would gain an entrepreneurial profit in addition to interest income. However, this assumes a state of disequilibrium, prompting wages to rise due to competitive forces. In equilibrium, capitalists earn interest, and workers are not "exploited" in Marx's sense, as they receive as wages the whole value of their labor.

6.2.11 The Use Theory

This theory emerged during the classical period as an evolution of productivity ideas. Menger (1976 [1871], p. 157) revisited and refined it, arguing that interest does not arise from the abstinence of capitalists or the exploitation of workers. Instead, he posits that interest is the price paid for the use of capital's services.

Production is inherently time-consuming and necessitates the availability of capital services over a specific duration. The availability of these services holds intrinsic value and, when exchanged for money, has a corresponding price: this price constitutes the interest on the invested capital. Furthermore, the longer these services are available, the higher the interest rate will be. Menger thus explains the discrepancy between the price of production factors (capital) and the price of the final product, which accounts for the existence of originary interest.

Böhm-Bawerk provides a compelling critique of this theory. In his analysis of goods, he demonstrates that a "relation" between an actor and a good does not qualify as a good in itself (see Sect. 2.1.8). While the power to utilize a good does represent a relationship between the actor and that good, this "power" is not an additional good. Essentially, Böhm-Bawerk argues that there is no separate good representing the ability to dispose of the factors of production beyond the factors themselves. The cost of utilizing these production factors over their usage period is already incorporated into their price. As such, the use theory fails to clarify the difference between the prices of products and production factors, and consequently does not account for the existence of interest.

In summary, after examining the various Austrian theories of interest, it is evident that the differences among these authors are significant and may be irreconcilable.

References

Clark, J. B. (1899). *The Distribution of Wealth. A Theory of Wages, Interest, and Profits*. Macmillan.
Dorfman, R. (1959). A Graphical Exposition of Böhm-Bawerk's Interest Theory. *Review of Economic Studies, February*, 153–158.
Fetter, F. (1900). Recent Discussion of the Capital Concept. In F. Fetter (1977) (pp. 33–73).
Fetter, F. (1901). The Passing of the Old Rent Concept. In F. Fetter (1977) (pp. 318–355).
Fetter, F. (1902). The "Roundabout Process" in the Interest Theory. In F. Fetter (1977) (pp. 172–191).
Fetter, F. (1914). *Interest Theories, Old and New*. In F. Fetter (1977) (pp. 226–255).
Fetter, F. (1927). *Interest Theory and Price Movements*. In F. Fetter (1977) (pp. 260–316).
Fetter, F. (1977). *Capital, Interest, and Rent. Essays in the Theory of Distribution*. Sheed Andrews and McMeel.
Garrison, R. W. (2001). *Time and Money. The Macroeconomics of the Capital Structure*. Routledge.
Hayek, F. A. (1941). *The Pure Theory of Capital*. The University of Chicago Press.
Horwitz, S. (2000). *Microfoundations and Macroeconomics. An Austrian Perspective*. Routledge.
Mankiw, G. N. (2010). *Principles of Economics*. Cengage Learning.
Menger, C. (1888). Zur Theorie des Kapitals. *Jahrbücher für Nationalökonomie und Statistik, 17*, 135–183.
Menger, C. (1976 [1871]). *Principles of Economics*. New York University Press.
Ricardo, D. (1951 [1817]). *On the Principles of Political Economy and Taxation*. Cambridge University Press.
Rothbard, M. N. (1962). *Man, Economy, and State. A Treatise on Economic Principles*. D. Van Nostrand.

Senior, N. (1836). *An Outline of the Science of Political Economy*. W. Clowes and Sons.
Skousen, M. (1990). *The Structure of Production*. New York University Press.
Smith, A. (1976 [1776]). *An Inquiry into the Nature and Causes of the Wealth of Nations*. The University of Chicago Press.
von Böhm-Bawerk, E. (1959a [1884]). *History and Critique of Interest Theories*. Libertarian Press.
von Böhm-Bawerk, E. (1959b [1889]). *Positive Theory of Capital*. Libertarian Press.
von Mises, L. (1981 [1922]). *Socialism. An Economic and Sociological Analysis*. LibertyClassics.
von Mises, L. (1998 [1949]). *Human Action. A Treatise on Economics*. Ludwig von Mises Institute.
Wicksell, K. (1954 [1893]). *Value, Capital and Rent*. George Allen and Unwin.

CHAPTER 7

Money and Its Purchasing Power

Abstract Building on Mises' pioneering work, this chapter delves into the historical evolution of money, examines various types of money—particularly the distinction between commodity and fiat money—and discusses the concept of economic calculation. Mises emphasizes that money is not a "neutral" medium but a key factor in determining prices through subjective valuations by economic actors. While supporting the quantity theory of money, he criticizes the simplistic interpretation presented by the "equation of exchange." The chapter also analyzes the redistributive impacts of changes in money supply, known as the "Cantillon Effect," and investigates purchasing power parity in relation with currency exchange rates.

Keywords Money • Economic calculation • Money prices • Quantity theory of money • Cantillon effect

Expanding upon the work of Menger (1976 [1871]) and Wieser (1910), Mises (1980 [1912]) successfully integrated money into the Austrian economic framework. His treatise on monetary issues remains a foundational text, now complemented by more recent work by Huerta de Soto (2006 [1998]), Salerno (2010), and Hülsmann (2008). The Austrian theory of money primarily focuses on monetary prices, fully recognizing

R. Fillieule, *The Austrian School of Economics*, Palgrave Studies in Austrian Economics,
https://doi.org/10.1007/978-3-031-83414-1_7

the monetary nature of prices themselves. Money prices are exchange rates between goods and money, driven by the subjective valuation that economic actors place on the money they hold. The use of money, therefore, directly influences the determination of *all* prices. Contrary to the view that money is merely a "veil" over barter transactions, the Austrian perspective asserts that money is never "neutral." Its purchasing power is shaped by the balance between the supply of money and individuals' demand for cash, as per the classic *quantity theory*, albeit revised in light of subjectivist and marginalist principles. Nevertheless, Mises strongly rejected the well-known "equation of exchange" ($MV = PT$) as an overly simplistic mathematical representation of the quantity theory of money.

7.1 The Concept of Money

7.1.1 The Function of Money

Money was neither invented nor created by political authority; it emerged organically from the development of the market economy. It enabled individuals to better satisfy their needs by overcoming the limitations of barter and promoting a more advanced division of labor (see Sect. 3.1.9). Mises, drawing on the ideas of Menger, concluded that the primary function of money is to facilitate market transactions by acting as a *common intermediary in exchanges*. Other functions often attributed to money—such as serving as a store of value, enabling credit transactions, or acting as a means of payment—are not separate functions but rather extensions of this core role (1980 [1912], p. 47).

Money presupposes exchange and thus requires private ownership, not only of consumer goods but, more importantly, of the factors of production. It would be irrelevant in economic systems not based on exchange, such as isolated domestic economies or collectivist systems.

7.1.2 Money as a Good

For Mises, money is a good, but it does not fall into the categories of either consumer goods or production factors. Instead, it belongs to a distinct third category: *medium of exchange*. The good used as money can simultaneously be a consumer good or a production factor. For example, gold, which has historically been used as money, also has uses in jewelry and as a component in electrical equipment. However, when used as money, gold functions neither as a consumer good (because it is transferred, not consumed) nor as a production factor (because increasing its quantity does not boost overall economic output).

7.1.3 *Types of Money*

Mises rejects the traditional distinction between metallic and paper money, considering it superficial. Instead, he identifies three types of currency (1980 [1912], p. 73, Hülsmann, 2008, Chap. 1):

1. *Commodity money*: A good that serves as money and can also be used for direct consumption. Historical examples include salt, cereals, and of course precious metals.
2. *Fiat money*: The good used as money derives its monetary character not from its physical characteristics but from legal designation. For instance, if a government mandates that only certain stamped gold coins can be used as money, this constitutes fiat money. Modern currencies such as the dollar and the euro are also fiat money.
3. *Credit money*: Debt instruments issued by individuals or legal entities that can be used as intermediaries in exchanges. If these instruments are convertible into money on demand and are considered entirely secure, they are treated as "money substitutes" (see next paragraph). However, if they carry some risk, they are subject to independent valuation and are categorized as "credit money."

7.1.4 *Money Substitutes*

Mises explains that monetary exchanges are often conducted not with actual money, but with debt securities representing an equivalent amount of money. As long as these securities are fully secure and convertible into real money on demand, they can circulate as intermediaries in exchanges, with successive holders not needing to convert them into actual money. These are known as "money substitutes." A classic example is banknotes in a gold-based monetary system. People use banknotes issued by banks, which are convertible into gold at the bank's counter. As long as these notes are considered perfectly safe, they serve as a substitute for gold as a medium of exchange. However, if doubts arise about their convertibility into gold, they cease to be substitutes for money. At that point, people begin to distinguish between the banknotes and money itself, and the notes may undergo a devaluation relative to actual money. In some countries, small coins may have also acted as money substitutes since their metal content was worth less than their face value, but they were still convertible into gold on demand by the central bank.

In his theory of credit and economic crises, Mises makes a key distinction between two types of money substitutes:

1. *Money certificates*: These are 100% backed by actual currency (gold or silver) held by the issuing bank.
2. *Fiduciary media*: This is only partially backed by currency, meaning the bank holds only a fraction of the gold or silver equivalent to the banknotes issued.

Mises' typology is illustrated in Fig. 7.1.

7.1.5 The Trend Toward Monetary Unification

The way money emerged as an institution explains the vast variety of goods that have served as currency throughout history. Each society with a sufficiently developed economy created its own currencies, shaped by factors such as the nature of its economic activities (e.g., hunting, herding, agriculture), its level of sedentarization, and the resources available in its

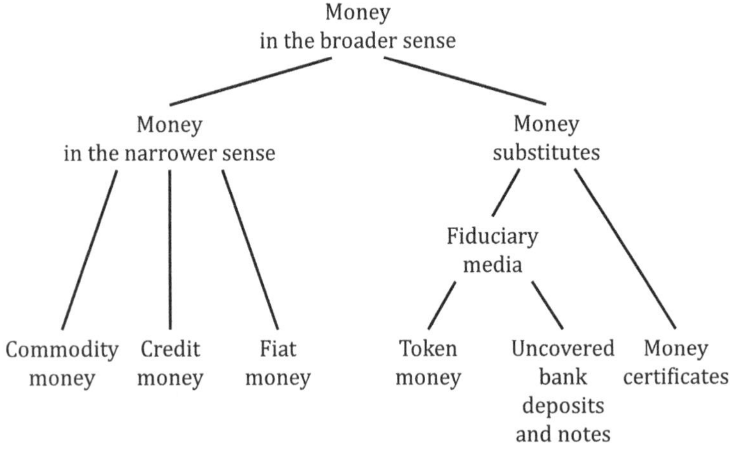

Fig. 7.1 Mises' typology of money (Mises, 1980 [1912], p. 526)

environment (such as shellfish in Polynesian societies or cocoa beans in South American societies).

When two monetary systems came into contact, money became essential for facilitating exchanges. Once again, the most "marketable" goods were chosen as intermediaries between the two systems. This led to a natural trend toward monetary unification as trade extended beyond the boundaries of individual societies.

Over time, economic development and the expansion of international trade resulted in the selection of precious metals like gold and silver as dominant currencies. These metals were chosen for their superior "exchangeability" due to their high value per unit volume, malleability, divisibility, durability, and ease of transport. Mises (1980 [1912], p. 46) believed that, given the inefficiencies of using multiple currencies, one—either gold or silver—would eventually have emerged as the sole global currency.

However, in the twentieth century, governments progressively *prohibited* the use of precious metals as money, replacing them with state-issued currencies with legal tender like today's euro and dollar. By thus becoming the producers of their own currency, governments gained the ability to create purchasing power out of nothing to finance their spending. They were also able to implement monetary policies, such as stimulating consumption (see Chap. 7). Without such government intervention, global monetary unification might have been achieved around one of the two precious metals. It is also quite possible that gold, silver, and other currencies used for smaller transactions continued to circulate alongside each other in a system of *monetary competition*. This system has its benefits, such as the ability to abandon a currency when its quality deteriorates (see Hülsmann 2008, p. 46, p. 76).

7.1.6 Money and Economic Calculation

In his three major works—on money, collectivism, and human action—Mises increasingly emphasizes the importance of economic calculation. His argument is that money, along with exchange and private property rights over the factors of production, is essential for the efficient operation of a developed economic system, as it allows individuals to perform the necessary calculations.

In a simple, isolated economy, such as that of Robinson Crusoe, an individual has little trouble assessing the relative value of the available resources. The production processes are short and few, making it possible for the actor to assign a subjective value to the different inputs, particularly labor, based on the value placed on the resulting consumer goods. For instance, if Crusoe wants to eat more meat, he knows how much extra labor to allocate to hunting, at the expense of gathering, fishing, or leisure.

However, the situation is entirely different in a complex, developed economic system, where production processes are numerous, long, and interconnected, and where most factors of production are convertible. In this case, producers need a tool to help them estimate, beforehand, whether the resources are being allocated in ways that best meet consumer demand. This tool also helps them verify afterward whether the allocation was efficient. To perform these calculations—estimating revenues, costs, capital, profits, and losses—an objective unit of measurement is needed. Since subjective values are ordinal and not cardinal (see Sect. 2.2.9), they cannot serve this purpose. Only money prices can provide the necessary information to calculate income and expenditure, allowing producers to determine if the resources, which could be used in alternative ways, are being wasted or not in the current production process. Without a system of monetary prices, subjective values cannot be applied to all interchangeable factors of production. Thus, exchange and private ownership of production factors are essential for economic calculation in a developed economy. This idea underpins Mises' famous critique of collectivism (see Sect. 9.3.4).

7.1.7 The Limits of Economic Calculation

The first limitation to economic calculation comes from fluctuations in the value of money. While such fluctuations are unavoidable, Mises argues that if the currency is "sound," meaning its value changes only slightly over time, these fluctuations do not significantly distort short- or medium-term economic calculations.

The second limitation is more fundamental: economic calculation only applies to goods that can be exchanged for money. Many goods, however, are not traded and therefore have no monetary price, which prevents them from being included in the economic calculation. For example, should a hydroelectric dam be built in a particular location? If the dam would ruin the landscape, economic calculation provides only a partial answer, as it cannot account for the non-monetary value of preserving the landscape. Nonetheless, it is possible to consider such factors and choose, for aesthetic reasons, not to build the dam. More broadly, choices between material goods and ideals—whether moral, spiritual, or aesthetic—cannot be resolved by economic calculation. Such decisions are made through direct judgment based on the subjective values of first-order goods. As Mises succinctly puts it, the choice between "bread and honor" cannot be settled by economic calculation alone (1935 [1920], pp. 98–101).

7.2 The Purchasing Power of Money

7.2.1 The Subjective Value of Money

The subjective value of a good refers to the importance an individual assigns to it in relation to other goods. Like any other good, money holds subjective value for the individual. Mises' views on the source of this value evolved between his 1912 treatise on money and his 1949 synthesis on human action (Hülsmann, 2007, p. 786).

In his earlier work, Mises explains that an individual assigns subjective value to a sum of money because it allows one to obtain other goods through exchange. This subjective value is therefore linked to the *objective* quantity of goods the money can buy—essentially, to its objective exchange value or, more simply, its purchasing power (Mises, 1980 [1912], p. 118).

In his later work, Mises shifts his focus to the concept of *cash holdings*. He argues that for the individual, cash holdings (a stock of money) have subjective value not merely because of the goods they can buy, but because they provide a specific service: the ability to have purchasing power readily available in an uncertain future. From this perspective, the subjective value of money still depends on its purchasing power—meaning a unit of money has more subjective value if it can buy more, all else being equal—but its value also stems from the unique role money plays in providing a reserve of purchasing power that can be accessed at any time in a world of radical uncertainty. In a perfectly certain future, money would be useless, and no one would want to hold any cash at all (see Sect. 7.2.5).

In any case, the main task of monetary theory is to explain how the purchasing power of money is determined, based on the subjective value assigned to it by economic actors.

7.2.2 The Historical Component of the Value of Money (Regression Theorem)

Mises' first point is that, unlike other goods, the purchasing power of money has a historical component (1980 [1912], p. 134). He illustrates this with the example of beer: today's price of beer is not directly influenced by yesterday's price, but this is not the case with money. As Wieser (1910) had already pointed out, there is a causal link between the purchasing power of money in one period and the next. Individuals form their preferences between goods and money based on the money prices they already know, specifically the prices from the previous period. Therefore, the money prices that emerge in the current period, which determine money's purchasing power today, are influenced by the money prices from the previous period.

In other words, the purchasing power—the objective exchange value—of money "today" depends on its purchasing power "yesterday," which in turn depends on its purchasing power "the day before yesterday," and so on. Mises calls this causal link the regression theorem (1998 [1949], pp. 405–406).

This regression logically traces back to the period when the good used as money was not yet serving as a medium of exchange but was valued for its utility as a consumer good or as a factor of production. At this point, the causal chain stops. All forms of commodity money can therefore be traced back to a time when they were valued for their intrinsic use rather than as money. This regression also explains why banknotes retain their value when their convertibility into precious metals like gold or silver is suspended by government intervention, allowing them to continue functioning as a medium of exchange.

7.2.3 The Foundation of the Subjectivist Theory of Money Prices

The money price of a good is determined in a market where money and goods are exchanged. Buyers and sellers make individual assessments, valuing units of money against units of goods to form their demand or supply. The aggregate of these demands and supplies determines the price of the good in terms of money. However, buyers and sellers must already be aware of the monetary prices of goods to carry out these valuations. This leads to an apparent circularity: money prices are determined based on the purchasing power of money, but this purchasing power is itself dependent on money prices.

Mises is considered the founder of the subjectivist theory of money because he was the first to resolve this paradox, successfully integrating money into the subjectivist and marginalist framework established by Menger. He demonstrated that this contradiction is only superficial (1980 [1912], p. 142). It vanishes once the historical aspect of money prices is considered. Economic actors evaluate their units of money based on the money prices from the previous period. In this way, they can form their current market supply and demand without contradiction by comparing the subjective value of a good with the subjective value of money. The prices established in this manner then play a role in determining the value of money—and thus the prices—in the next period. A continuous process is created in which the prices of the previous period explain the value of money in the current period, which explains prices in the current period, which in turn explain the value of money in the next period, and so on. This explanation of money prices, situated within Austrian value theory, avoids both circular reasoning and infinite regression (Mises, 1998 [1949], pp. 405–406; Rothbard, 1962, p. 235).

7.2.4 *The Quantity Theory of Money*

The "quantity theory" of money has deep roots in economic thought, long predating the Classical period of the nineteenth century. For Mises, however, it remains the fundamental theory for understanding the purchasing power of money. While he opposed the mechanistic and holistic interpretations of the theory (see Sect. 7.2.12), he retained its core insight, which is based on the law of supply and demand: the purchasing power of money depends on the balance between the supply of and demand for money. If the money supply increases while demand stays constant, its purchasing power will tend to decrease, and vice versa. If demand for money rises while supply remains unchanged, its purchasing power will tend to increase, and conversely.

7.2.5 *The Demand for Money*

For Mises, individual money demand is essentially a demand for cash balances. As with any other good, market demand for money in a given period is the sum of individual demands. The amount of money an individual holds at any moment is not simply leftover, unspent cash; it is the result of a conscious decision, a trade-off between spending and retaining money (Mises, 1998 [1949], p. 399; Salin, 1990, p. 136).

The underlying reason for holding cash is *uncertainty* about the future. In a perfectly predictable world, economic actors would have no need for cash balances, as all transactions could be foreseen with certainty. If no one held cash, this would imply that money would cease to exist within the economic system. In the hypothetical (and unrealistic) scenario where the future is certain, money would have no function and would disappear (Mises, 1998 [1949], p. 414).

7.2.6 *The Supply of Money*

The money supply is the total stock of money available in the economic system. Mises refers to this as the "broad" sense of the money supply (see Fig. 7.1). The composition of this stock varies depending on the banking system:

- If bank reserves are fully backed (non-fractional), meaning banks issue currency certificates that are 100% backed by reserves, then the stock of money corresponds to the quantity of gold held for monetary purposes.
- If bank reserves are fractional, the total money supply includes both the amount of physical gold (money in the strict sense) and the quantity of uncovered substitutes (fiduciary media).
- In our current system of state-issued fiat money, the money supply consists of central banknotes and customers' deposit accounts, which corresponds to the standard monetary aggregate M1.

Rothbard (1997 [1978], p. 346) argues that the concept of the money supply should be expanded to include all instruments convertible into money on demand at a fixed rate, such as savings accounts and bonds (at their redemption price). However, in a later work, he redefines the money supply as the sum of central banknotes and deposit account balances (2008 [1983], p. 132).

7.2.7 The Convergence Toward Monetary Equilibrium

Mises (1998 [1949]) does not develop a detailed theory explaining how the purchasing power of money converges to an equilibrium value. Instead, he simply states that the purchasing power of money in any given period is determined by the "monetary relation"—the interaction between money supply and demand. This demand is partly influenced by the purchasing power of money from the previous period, according to his regression theorem.

Rothbard (1962, p. 662), on the other hand, presents a more detailed model that describes how the purchasing power of money converges to an equilibrium level using a "total demand-stock" analysis. It is unclear whether Rothbard's theory aligns perfectly with Mises' ideas, but that question will not be explored here.

Let us consider a non-monetary good, *A*. Its "total demand" for the current period consists of two types of demand:

- *Exchange demand*, which is the usual concept of demand used in market models: the quantities of good *A* that individuals want to buy at various possible monetary prices (assuming all else remains equal).
- *Reserve demand*, which refers to the quantities of good *A* that its current owners want to keep at different price points. For example, an actor who owns 12 units of good *A* may want to keep 8 units if the price per unit is $1 but would keep only 5 units if the price rises to $2.

These demand concepts can be extended to money. For money, exchange demand represents the quantity of money that economic agents want to acquire by selling their goods (such as labor) at different purchasing power levels. Total demand for money in a given period is the sum of exchange demand and reserve demand, plus, in the case of commodity money, any demand for non-monetary uses.

Both exchange and reserve demand for money decrease as the purchasing power of money increases. When money's purchasing power rises, individuals need less of it to exchange for goods, and they also wish to hold smaller reserves for future spending. Consequently, the total demand for money *decreases*, as it is the sum of these two decreasing functions. The money supply, however, is fixed—it is the total amount of money available in the system and is not influenced by changes in purchasing power, so it is represented as a *vertical line*.

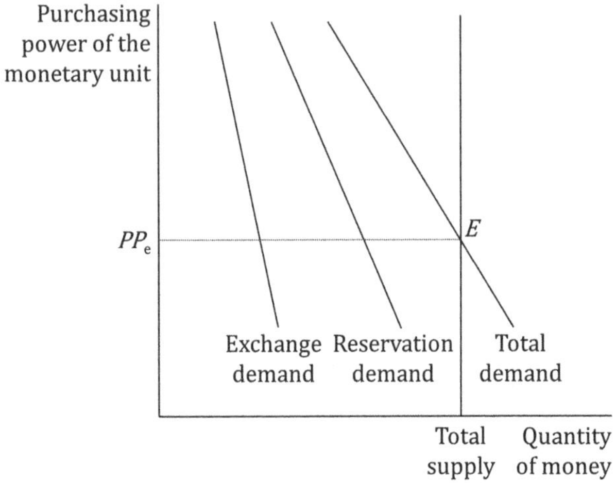

Fig. 7.2 Equilibrium purchasing power of money (after Rothbard, 1962, p. 667)

In Fig. 7.2, we see how money supply and demand relate to the purchasing power of money, which is represented on the vertical axis as if it were a simple numerical variable (a necessary but significant simplification). When the purchasing power of money is above its equilibrium point, the total demand for money is lower than its supply. As a result, people spend more money, driving up the demand—and therefore the prices—of goods. This causes the purchasing power of money to fall, bringing it back to equilibrium. Conversely, when the purchasing power of money is below equilibrium, it rises toward equilibrium through the opposite process: people prefer to hold larger cash balances, leading them to spend less; this reduced spending lowers prices, which increases the purchasing power of money.

7.2.8 *The Effects of Changes in the Supply of or Demand for Money on Its Purchasing Power*

When the supply of money increases, individuals find themselves with larger amounts of money compared to their other goods. As a result, the marginal utility of money tends to decrease. Consequently, expenditure rises, which increases the monetary demand for goods. This, in turn, drives up monetary prices, representing a decrease in the purchasing power of money.

If demand for money increases individuals choose to hold onto larger amounts of cash (increased hoarding). This results in decreased monetary expenditure, a reduction in demand for other goods, and a subsequent decline in monetary prices, that is, an increase in the purchasing power of money. Here, we see the classic effects of the law of supply and demand, specifically the quantitative theory of money (Mises, 1980 [1912], p. 161, p. 175).

These dynamics can also be illustrated in Rothbard's diagram (see Fig. 7.2). An increase in the total supply of money leads to a decrease in equilibrium purchasing power, while an increase in total demand for money results in higher purchasing power.

Significant changes in the money supply can influence its demand as people anticipate substantial fluctuations in purchasing power. For example, if the money supply increases rapidly, prices are likely to rise quickly as well. If individuals expect this price increase to persist, they may reduce their demand for money. The longer they hold onto a unit of money, the more its value diminishes (meaning the quantity of goods that unit can buy decreases). Thus, a sustained increase in the money supply can lead to a reduction in the demand for money, further contributing to a decline in its purchasing power (Mises, 1998 [1949], p. 424).

7.2.9 *The Influence of the Real Sphere*

Fluctuations in the purchasing power of money can stem from the monetary sphere, as we have just discussed, but they can also arise from the real sphere, particularly on the production side. If the overall supply of goods increases—perhaps due to technological advancements—these additional goods will be offered for sale in exchange for money. All else being equal, this increase in supply will typically cause unit prices to fall, thereby increasing the purchasing power of money. Conversely, if production and the overall supply of goods decrease, prices are likely to rise, leading to a decline in the purchasing power of money (see Sect. 8.1.3). In short, an increase in the money supply is "inflationary," while economic growth is "deflationary."

7.2.10 The Redistributive Effect of an Increase in the Quantity of Money (Cantillon Effect)

When the quantity of money increases—whether through the production of commodity money or the issuance of fiat money—the purchasing power of money tends to decline, all else being equal. However, this decline does not happen instantaneously; rather, it unfolds gradually as the new money circulates within the economic system.

The introduction of new money benefits the first economic players who receive it. These individuals now possess a larger amount of money, causing their marginal utility of money to decrease. As a result, they are likely to spend part of this additional income on certain goods, leading to an increase in demand and subsequently higher prices for those goods. The sellers of these goods then receive the new money, which they will also spend on other goods, driving demand and prices higher in those markets as well. This process continues, but its effects are strongest at the initial points of entry for the new money and diminish as more individuals receive and spend it.

This diffusion process clearly favors the first recipients of the new money, as they can purchase goods at pre-increase prices. In contrast, those who receive the new money later must pay higher prices before they can enjoy the benefits of the increased monetary income, resulting in a temporary decline in their standard of living as the process unfolds (Mises, 1980 [1912], pp. 161–162). Hayek (1931) traces this theory back to eighteenth-century economist Richard Cantillon, identifying the phenomenon as the "Cantillon effect."

7.2.11 Money Is Never "Neutral"

Not only are the effects of changes in the money supply (or demand) not instantaneous, but they are also not uniform—and they can never be. A neutral currency would theoretically allow changes in purchasing power to lead to proportional changes in all prices without impacting production and consumption activities, which would remain unchanged. For instance, if the quantity of money were to double, all prices would double as well, leaving the "real" aspects of the economy unaffected.

However, Mises (1998 [1949], p. 413) argues that money can never be neutral. Each individual reacts differently to a change in their monetary stock, and their responses vary based on their unique situations and subjective preferences. This results in adjustments in monetary expenditure that differ in direction and intensity among individuals. Such varied reactions inevitably influence production, favoring certain goods and their producers at the expense of others. The same applies to individual variations in money demand. Consequently, changes in the monetary sphere always spill over into the real sphere, making it impossible for money to be neutral.

7.2.12 *Critique of the Equation of Exchange*

The "equation of exchange" is a mathematical formulation of the quantitative theory of money, popularized in the early twentieth century by Fisher (1911, pp. 26–27) in the following form:

$$MV = PT.$$

In this equation, M represents the quantity of money, V the velocity of money (the average number of times a unit of money is exchanged within a specific period), P the general price level, and T the number of transactions carried out during that period (for instance, over a year). Fisher assumes that V and T remain constant and concludes that if the quantity of money M doubles, the price level P will also double, resulting in a halving of the purchasing power of money.

Mises completely rejected this equation, arguing that it is fundamentally flawed due to his holistic view of economic phenomena. He emphasized that exchange rates are based on the subjective evaluations of the individuals involved in transactions. Consequently, a broad relationship like the equation of exchange cannot adequately explain variations in the purchasing power of money. Additionally, Mises contended that the mechanical implications of this equation—such as the assertion that doubling the quantity of money halves its purchasing power—are strictly incorrect, as money is never neutral (Mises, 1980 [1912], pp. 166–168).

7.2.13 *Long-Term Influences on Money Demand and Supply*

In the very long term, the demand for money tends to rise as more individuals participate in the monetary economic system. As the division of labor and monetary exchange replace self-sufficiency (autarky), or simply as the population grows, the need for money increases, leading to a higher total demand for cash (Mises, 1980 [1912], p. 174). This upward pressure on demand is counterbalanced by the development of the clearinghouse system, which allows money transfers between customers of different banks to be settled at the end of a period rather than for each transaction. As a result, many of these transactions offset each other, requiring significantly fewer movements of money.

On the supply side, variations in *commodity currencies* are quite limited. For instance, the quantity of gold increases only slightly each year (approximately 2%), which can only have a marginal downward effect on the purchasing power of gold coins (Skousen, 1996 [1977], p. 86). However, with the shift from gold and silver currencies to state-backed *fiat currencies*, there are no longer any physical limitations on the increase in the money supply. Central banks can create substantial amounts of reserve money, which banks can then multiply through fractional reserve banking. It can be demonstrated that if banks are only required to hold a fraction x of money in reserve against demand deposits, they can increase the money supply by a factor of $1/x$; for instance, at a current reserve ratio of 10% (where $x = 0.10$), banks can multiply the quantity of reserve money by 10.

The cumulative effect of these practices throughout the twentieth century has been a significant decline in the purchasing power of currencies across the globe. Using the consumer price index, Hazlitt (1978, p. 20) notes that the dollar, despite being one of the more stable currencies, lost three-quarters of its purchasing power between 1940 and 1976. Hayek (1990 [1976], pp. 136–137) discusses what he terms the "destruction of paper money," observing that between 1950 and 1975, various national currencies lost between 40% and 99% of their value: for example, the US and Swiss currencies lost 57%, France lost 75%, the UK lost 78%, and several Latin American countries, such as Chile, Argentina, and Brazil, experienced losses exceeding 99%.

7.2.14 Changes in the Purchasing Power of Money and Interest Rates

This section focuses solely on the long-term effects of changes in the purchasing power of money on the originary interest rate. Short-term effects, particularly those arising from a rapid decline in purchasing power due to inflationary credit expansion, are addressed in the context of cycle theory (see Sect. 8.2.3).

According to Mises (1980 [1912]), changes in the value of money do not directly affect the *real* interest rate. However, they can have an indirect impact. When the purchasing power of money fluctuates—whether due to changes in money supply or demand—redistribution occurs (Cantillon effect). If this redistribution favors capitalists at the expense of other economic agents, savings are likely to increase, leading to a decrease in the interest rate. Conversely, if redistribution adversely affects capitalists, savings are likely to decrease, causing the interest rate to rise. Nonetheless, there is no reason to favor one scenario over the other, leading to the conclusion that variations in the purchasing power of money do not systematically affect the originary long-term real interest rate.

In contrast, the *nominal* interest rate is influenced by changes in the purchasing power of money. For instance, if prices rise by an average of 3% per year, selling prices will also be approximately 3% higher a year later, which will be reflected in the annual nominal interest rate. If the real interest rate is 4%, the nominal interest rate would thus be approximately 4% + 3% = 7% (Reisman, 1996, p. 763).

Hülsmann (2009) offers a nuanced perspective on the Misesian view by distinguishing between commodity money and fiat money. He argues that, in the case of commodity money, changes in the demand for money have a systematic effect on interest rates, leading to a corresponding variation in the equilibrium interest rate. For example, if the currency is gold and the demand for money increases, money prices tend to decline. This results in increased profitability for gold production, as the price of gold compared to other goods rises—meaning the same amount of gold can purchase more goods—while production costs decrease (since all money prices, especially those related to gold production, tend to fall). Meanwhile, the average profitability of other goods (the originary interest rate) remains unchanged. Consequently, capital will be reallocated toward gold production, causing the rate of return in that sector to fall while the rate of return in other production areas increases due to the outflow of capital. Thus, the new equilibrium interest rate will be higher than the initial rate. Therefore, in the context of commodity money, the interest rate moves in the same direction as the demand for money. In contrast, this effect does not manifest with fiat money, which can be produced at little to no cost.

7.2.15 The Purchasing Power Parity Theory

Let us consider two distinct currencies, Currency *A* and Currency *B*, used in two different countries or possibly alongside each other in the same territory. Producers, including exporters and importers, investors, and travelers exchange these currencies, creating an *exchange rate* between them.

This exchange rate tends to align with what is known as their "purchasing power parity," a term popularized by Cassel (Mises, 1980 [1912], p. 207). At this parity, individuals can purchase the same quantities of goods using either a specified amount of Currency *A* or the equivalent amount of Currency *B* obtained through exchange. In simpler terms, the exchange rate between the currencies corresponds to the ratio of their respective purchasing powers. For instance, if one unit of Currency *A* can buy two units of a good or a basket of goods, while one unit of Currency *B* can buy four units of the same good or basket, then the purchasing power of Currency *B* is double that of Currency *A*. Consequently, at parity, one unit of Currency *B* would be exchanged for two units of Currency *A*.

When the exchange rate deviates from this parity, individuals will engage in trade-offs to restore the balance in line with the purchasing power ratio. Suppose that one currency is ***overvalued*** compared to the other. For example, its purchasing power is double that of the other currency, but its exchange rate is triple—meaning one unit of the overvalued currency is exchanged for three units of the ***undervalued*** currency (when it only has a double purchasing power). In this scenario, individuals have an incentive to exchange their goods for the overvalued currency, then trade that currency for the undervalued one, and finally purchase goods with the resulting amount. This series of exchanges allows them to acquire more goods than they initially had. During this process, the demand for the undervalued currency increases while the demand for the overvalued one decreases, gradually reducing the discrepancy in value until it aligns with the purchasing power parity (see Rothbard, 1962, p. 725, for a more detailed analysis).

Thus, the exchange rate between two currencies tends to converge to the parity of their respective purchasing powers. When one currency loses value relative to another, it signifies a relative decline in its purchasing power, often as a result of inflationary policies. For example, if the supply of Currency *A* increases due to monetary creation in country *A*, its purchasing power diminishes compared to that of the foreign Currency *B* (whose supply has remained stable). Over time, the exchange rate will reflect this new parity, indicating a depreciation of Currency *A* relative to Currency *B*. Mises firmly opposes the notion that the decline in a national currency's value against others is caused by an "unfavorable" balance of payments, i.e., by the fact that country *A* imports more goods from *B* than it exports (1980 [1912], p. 282 and p. 286).

References

Fisher, I. (1911). *The Purchasing Power of Money. Its Determination and Relation to Credit Interest and Crises.* Macmillan.

Hayek, F. A. (1931). *Prices and Production.* George Routledge and Sons.

Hayek, F. A. (1990 [1976]). *Denationalisation of Money: The Argument Refined. An Analysis of the Theory and Practice of Concurrent Currencies.* The Institute of Economic Affairs.

Hazlitt, H. (1978). *The Inflation Crisis, and How to Resolve It.* Arlington House.

Huerta de Soto, J. (2006 [1998]). *Money, Bank Credit, and Economic Cycles.* Ludwig von Mises Institute.

Hülsmann, J. G. (2007). *Mises. The Last Knight of Liberalism.* Ludwig von Mises Institute.

Hülsmann, J. G. (2008). *The Ethics of Money Production.* Ludwig von Mises Institute.

Hülsmann, J. G. (2009). The Demand for Money and the Time-Structure of Production. In J. G. Hülsmann & S. Kinsella (Eds.), *Property, Freedom, Society. Essays in Honor of Hans-Hermann Hoppe* (pp. 309–324). Ludwig von Mises Institute.

Menger, C. (1976 [1871]). *Principles of Economics.* New York University Press.

Reisman, G. (1996). *Capitalism. A Treatise on Economics.* Jameson Books.

Rothbard, M. N. (1962). *Man, Economy, and State. A Treatise on Economic Principles.* D. Van Nostrand.

Rothbard, M. N. (1997 [1978]). Austrian Definitions of the Supply of Money. In M. N. Rothbard (Ed.), *The Logic of Action I. Money, Method and the Austrian School* (pp. 337–349). Edward Elgar.

Rothbard, M. N. (2008 [1983]). *The Mystery of Banking.* Ludwig von Mises Institute.

Salerno, J. T. (2010). *Money, Sound and Unsound.* Ludwig von Mises Institute.

Salin, P. (1990). *La Vérité sur la Monnaie.* Odile Jacob.

Skousen, M. (1996 [1977]). *Economics of a Pure Gold Standard.* The Foundation for Economic Education.

von Mises, L. (1935 [1920]). Economic Calculation in the Socialist Commonwealth. In F. A. Hayek (Ed.), *Collectivist Economic Planning. Critical Studies on the Possibilities of Socialism* (pp. 87–130). George Routledge & Sons.

von Mises, L. (1980 [1912]). *The Theory of Money and Credit.* LibertyClassics.

von Mises, L. (1998 [1949]). *Human Action. A Treatise on Economics.* Ludwig von Mises Institute.

von Wieser, F. (1910). *Der Geldwert und seine geschichtliche Veränderungen.* Zeitschrift fur Volkswirtschaft.

CHAPTER 8

Inflation and Cycle

Abstract This chapter defines inflation as an increase in the money supply beyond the increase that occurs or would have occurred in commodity money. It critiques inflation on account of its arbitrary redistributive effects, distortion of profit calculations, and capital misallocation. Austrian economists advocate against fiat money systems and favor instead commodity-backed currencies that generate long-term slow deflationary tendencies in prices. The Austrian Business Cycle Theory (ABCT) then explains how credit expansion artificially lowers interest rates, causing unsustainable booms followed by inevitable crises and recessions. Historical examples, including the Great Depression and subprime crisis, illustrate this theory.

Keywords Inflation • Monetary institutions • Austrian business cycle theory • Great Depression

Mises' monetary work (1980 [1912], 1978) was fundamentally opposed to inflation and government-led money creation from the very beginning. He believed such policies would disrupt the price system, lead to economic impoverishment, and create imbalances that would eventually trigger

R. Fillieule, *The Austrian School of Economics*, Palgrave Studies in Austrian Economics,
https://doi.org/10.1007/978-3-031-83414-1_8

crises. This opposition became a defining feature of the Austrian School, which ultimately advocated a remedy that may seem radical today: a return to commodity-backed money.

8.1 Inflation: Definitions, Causes, Consequences, and Remedies

8.1.1 *"Austrian" Definitions*

In the Austrian economic framework, inflation and deflation are inherently monetary phenomena, defined, respectively, as the creation and destruction of money. Mises provides the following theoretical definitions (1980 [1912], p. 272):

- *Inflation* is an increase in the quantity of money (broadly defined) that is not matched by a corresponding rise in the demand for money, leading to a decline in its purchasing power (i.e., a rise in prices).
- *Deflation* is a contraction in the money supply without a proportional decrease in the demand for money, resulting in an increase in its purchasing power (i.e., a fall in prices).

Rothbard offers a different perspective (1962, p. 940, p. 942). For him, inflation occurs when the money supply grows faster than the quantity of gold (or faster than the amount of commodity money that would be used in a free market). Conversely, deflation happens when the money supply either contracts or grows more slowly than the quantity of gold—both of which can only occur if inflation has previously taken place.

To maintain consistency throughout this chapter, ***Rothbard's definition will be used***, as it has been adopted by Hazlitt (1978, p. 11), Reisman (1996, p. 895), and Hülsmann (2008a, p. 85). However, this definition is not universally accepted, as Horwitz (2000, p. 104, p. 142) uses the Misesian definitions of inflation and deflation, treating them as disruptions in monetary equilibrium.

While the previous chapter focused on the purchasing power of money, this chapter will discuss inflation in terms of the level of prices: a higher overall level of prices corresponds to a lower purchasing power of money, and vice versa.

8.1.2 Inflation and Price Increases

Inflation is commonly defined in both the media and economics textbooks as a general rise in prices. However, it is important to note that the Austrian School does not equate inflation with rising prices. According to Rothbard's (as well as Mises') definition, inflation leads to higher prices, *everything else equal.* However, in specific historical contexts where other factors are not held constant, it is possible to have *inflation without price increases*, and *price increases without inflation*—understood here as an increase in the money supply exceeding the growth of gold reserves.

- *Inflation without price increases*: If inflation is moderate while production increases significantly, for example, due to great technological advancements, then the price increases caused by inflation can be more than offset by the fall in prices resulting from the greater supply of goods. This occurred in the United States during the 1920s: wholesale and consumer prices remained relatively stable because the inflation-driven price rise was counterbalanced by the effects of strong economic growth (Rothbard 1983 [1963], p. 154).
- *Price increases without inflation*: In very rare historical cases, prices can rise without inflation. If prices tend to increase while the money supply does not grow faster than the supply of gold, this could be due to either an overall decrease in production or a drop in the demand for money. However, these factors are usually temporary and limited, and neither can account for a sustained and significant rise in prices.

8.1.3 Cost-Driven "Inflation"?

One of the most simplistic explanations for a general rise in prices is the notion that greedy capitalist producers raise prices to increase their profits, known as "profit-push inflation." However, this argument is flawed. Producers typically set prices to maximize their income from the start, so raising prices further would likely reduce their income, not increase it (Rothbard, 1977 [1970], p. 89). Therefore, this explanation cannot account for widespread price increases.

Similarly unsatisfactory are the common "cost-push inflation" theories, which attribute rising prices to increasing production costs (Reisman, 1996, pp. 907–915). The most common version of this is "wage-push inflation." If trade unions successfully increase wages across all sectors, producers may have to lay off workers due to higher labor costs, and the quantity of labor in the economic system falls. As a result, overall production decreases, and prices rise, all else being equal. Another variant is "crisis-push inflation," such as the sudden scarcity of a key resource (e.g., oil during the 1973 crisis) or a crop failure. In all of these cases, reduced production leads to higher prices.

However, these forms of "inflation" are limited by their intermittent and exceptional nature. None of them can produce a lasting rise in prices. Only substantial and repeated increases in the money supply can lead to a sustained and significant devaluation of money.

8.1.4 Causes of Inflation

According to Rothbard's definition, inflation is not caused by the production of commodity money, such as gold mining, but by the *creation* of additional money.

In a *commodity money system*, where gold, for example, serves as money in the narrow sense, banks cause inflation by issuing *fiduciary money*—whether legally or not—without sufficient backing (i.e., by reducing their reserve ratio, or the proportion of gold covering their deposit accounts).

In a *fiat money system*, like the one we have today, *central banks* are responsible for generating inflation (Hazlitt, 1978, pp. 118–120) through several mechanisms:

- Printing more central bank notes;
- Allowing commercial banks to reduce their reserve requirements, enabling them to create more money based on their existing reserves;
- Lowering the discount interest rate, which is the rate at which banks can borrow from the central bank;
- Creating money out of nothing (*ex nihilo*) and injecting it into the economy by purchasing government bonds; this *open market policy* is also known as "debt monetization": money is created to buy public debt.

The last method is the one most frequently used by central banks today. It increases the amount of reserves available to commercial banks, which can then multiply the quantity of money by further fractioning these additional reserves.

8.1.5 Consequences of Inflation

Beyond the decline in the purchasing power of money, Mises outlines three key consequences of inflation (1980 [1912], pp. 226–243):

1. *Wealth redistribution*: Inflation redistributes wealth in favor of the first recipients of newly created money, to the detriment of those who receive it last (on this Cantillon effect, see Sect. 7.2.11).
2. *Impact on creditors and debtors*: If the decline in the value of money is unexpected or underestimated, debtors benefit at the expense of creditors because they repay loans with money that has lost value. However, if the decline is anticipated, creditors will demand higher interest rates to compensate for the loss in purchasing power, preventing redistribution in favor of borrowers.
3. *Distortion of profit calculation*: When currency depreciates, calculating profit—which involves subtracting past costs from current revenues—becomes distorted. This is because revenues are recorded in a currency that has lost value compared to the time when the costs were incurred. As a result, profits tend to be overstated, increasing the risk of capital consumption (see below).

8.1.6 Economic Harms of Inflation

Mises and his followers, including Hayek (1931), Rothbard (1990 [1963]), Sennholz (1977), Hazlitt (1978), Reisman (1996), Huerta de Soto (2006 [1998]), and Hülsmann (2008a), are deeply critical of inflation for two key reasons. First, they argue that inflation is *the root cause of the recurrent economic crises* faced by capitalist economies—a point that will be explored in the next section. Second, they believe that inflation *impedes capital accumulation* and thus stifles economic progress by:

- *Capital consumption (overconsumption)*: When producers fail to account for the fact that inflation distorts their economic calculations, they may overestimate their profits and inadvertently consume part of their capital, believing they are preserving it. This overconsumption is only temporary, as it comes at the expense of future consumption (Mises, 1980 [1912], p. 235).
- *A surtax on capital*: When corporate profits are taxed at a fixed rate (e.g., 30%), inflation-induced overvaluation of profits leads to an

effective tax rate higher than 30%. If investors do not adjust their consumption accordingly, this excessive taxation reduces productive investment and shifts resources toward government consumption (Mises, 1980 [1912], p. 236; Reisman, 1996, p. 931).

- *Favoring debtors over creditors*: When inflation is poorly anticipated or underestimated, debtors benefit at the expense of creditors, who are repaid with money that has lost purchasing power.
- *Undermining safe investments*: Inflation turns traditionally safe investments, such as bonds, life insurance policies, and treasury bills, into subpar ones. These investments offer fixed interest payments, which are not adjusted for inflation, so unanticipated declines in the purchasing power of money directly erode the value of these repayments (Reisman, 1996, p. 930).

Moreover, the institutions that enable inflation—such as fiat money and the central bank as the lender of last resort—create significant *moral hazards*. On the one hand, political authorities are tempted to exploit their power to create unlimited money, risking abuse until hyperinflation or currency collapse occurs. On the other hand, banks and even other companies, knowing the government can bail them out through money creation, are incentivized to take excessive risks. Therefore, the institutions of inflation encourage reckless and irresponsible decision-making in the financial system (Hülsmann, 2006).

8.1.7 Other Harms of Inflation

Hülsmann (2008a, Chap. 13) argues that inflationary institutions and policies—such as fiat money, central banks, and "open market" operations—have consequences that extend far beyond the economic sphere. These effects permeate the moral, political, and cultural realms.

- *Moral implications*: Hülsmann contends that paper currencies are inherently immoral because they result from a massive violation of private property rights. Governments force citizens to use fiat currency, which they might otherwise reject if they had the freedom to choose commodity-based money.
- *Unfair redistribution*: Inflation creates arbitrary and unjust redistribution of wealth, particularly through the Cantillon effect. Central banks' "open market" policies disproportionately benefit commercial

banks, allowing them to profit from money they create out of nothing in the form of credit.

- *Hidden taxation*: When governments use newly created money to fund expenditures, they compete with other buyers for goods, effectively imposing a hidden tax. This process allows governments to acquire more goods at the expense of citizens without their knowledge or consent, bypassing democratic oversight (see also Mises, 1980 [1912], p. 468).
- *War financing*: This hidden inflationary tax has historically been used during wars (e.g., both World Wars) to obscure the true costs of these conflicts from the public. It also helps prolong military engagements by providing governments with financial resources that might not have received democratic approval.
- *One-sided empowerment of financial institutions*: Inflation gives financial institutions, especially banks, disproportionate power. Not only do they enrich themselves by profiting from money creation, but inflation also forces others to rely more heavily on their services. In an inflationary environment, hoarding money is not in households' best interest because the value of cash diminishes over time. As a result, people are pushed to invest their savings through financial institutions. This increased focus on money fosters materialism, while debt—and the accompanying financial dependence and risk of over-indebtedness—replaces autonomy and personal responsibility.

8.1.8 "Forced Savings"

Inflation can encourage capital accumulation in one specific case: through the mechanism of "forced saving," a concept already familiar to Classical economists (Hayek, 1939 [1932], p. 194). When newly created money is lent to businesses, it causes a redistribution from consumption to investment, which can promote capital accumulation and increase production.

According to Austrian economists, this phenomenon of forced saving reveals the grain of truth in inflationary government policies. However, they argue that even if forced savings could theoretically counterbalance the negative effects of inflation, it is highly unlikely in practice. At best, forced savings might somewhat mitigate the harmful impacts of inflation (Mises, 1980 [1912], pp. 252–253; Reisman, 1996, p. 937; Huerta de Soto, 2006 [1998], pp. 409–413).

8.1.9 False Solutions to Inflation

Due to their deep opposition to inflation, Austrian economists, since the time of Mises, have been keenly interested in methods to limit or get rid of it. They dismiss *price controls* as entirely ineffective and harmful. Price controls merely address the consequences of inflation—rising prices—rather than its root causes, and they create additional distortions in the economy (see Sect. 9.1.3).

What about *stabilizing the value of money*? Mises argued that such a policy faces insurmountable challenges. First, measuring the purchasing power of money involves an element of arbitrariness. Second, any efforts to counter fluctuations in money's value would require quick and precise interventions, which is impractical. Furthermore, giving the government discretionary power over the value of money poses a significant risk, as it could easily shift from stabilizing the currency to promoting inflation.

Moreover, stabilizing the value of money during a period of rapid economic growth would require the central bank to expand credit aggressively, which could destabilize the economy and lead to a crisis (see Sect. 8.2). Variations in the value of money are unavoidable. Even though they cannot be entirely eliminated, they should be limited by appropriate institutions, particularly by using metallic currencies (Mises, 1980 [1912], p. 269).

8.1.10 Monetary Institutions for a "Sound" Currency

Austrian economists completely reject the current monetary system, which centers around a central bank monopolizing the issuance of fiat currency. They argue that this setup allows excessive government control and manipulation, increasing the risk of inflation. To foster economic progress and avoid crises, they advocate for a "sound" currency. Their solution is straightforward: a return to *commodity-based currencies*, particularly gold and silver.

Even without a central bank and with gold and silver as the main forms of currency, two different banking systems are possible. The key difference lies in whether banks are allowed or not to create fiduciary money ("free banking" vs. "money warehouses").

In both systems, banks would compete to attract demand deposits from the public, issuing money substitutes like banknotes and conducting transfers via checks or bank cards. Under a "free banking" system, banks are contractually required to *convert on demand* these money substitutes into commodity money (such as gold or silver). A person holding a banknote or check issued by a bank could exchange it for the equivalent amount of gold or silver at any time.

In a "money warehouse" system, banks are required to hold the *full amount* of their customers' deposits in reserve. For example, if a customer deposits 3 ounces of gold and 8 ounces of silver, those exact quantities must remain in the bank's vault until the customer chooses to withdraw them.

Hayek (1990 [1976]) proposed an alternative institutional model: the *competitive issuance* of fiat currencies by private financial institutions. These institutions would have a strong incentive to maintain the value of their currencies—typically pegged to a basket of natural resources—since losing stability would result in losing customers. However, this proposal will not be explored further in this discussion.

8.1.11 Free Banking (Fractional Reserves)

In a free banking system, banks are legally permitted to create and lend fiduciary money, allowing them to fractionalize their commodity currency reserves at their discretion. The more a bank creates fiduciary money while others do not, the more it attracts withdrawal requests from customers of other banks (to whom its own customers make payments). As a result, the bank's stock of commodity money diminishes, weakening its ability to convert its money substitutes on demand and increasing the risk of bankruptcy. This principle of *adverse clearings* is examined in detail by Mises (1998 [1949], p. 434) and Selgin (1988, p. 40).

There is a significant difference of opinion regarding the functioning of the free banking system (Rothbard, 1988, p. 234). For Mises (1998 [1949], p. 443), prudence encourages banks to strictly limit their money creation. If they do not, they may struggle to meet their contractual obligations for convertibility on demand, jeopardize their reputation, and risk bankruptcy in the event of a sudden and large demand for withdrawals of gold or silver. Historically, free banks may have maintained relatively low reserve ratios because they anticipated government assistance in case of trouble (a moral hazard). However, if they know they cannot rely at all on government support, they are likely to adopt a much higher reserve ratio as a precaution, though it may not necessarily reach 100% (Salerno, 1993, p. 140; Huerta de Soto, 2006 [1998], p. 716, argues that Mises advocated for a gold money system with 100% reserves).

Conversely, advocates of free banking, such as Selgin (1988), argue that this system allows for greater flexibility than the strict requirement of 100% reserves, enabling adjustments to the money supply based on monetary needs. For instance, if the demand for money increases, a pure gold standard (with 100% reserves) would raise the value of money, potentially diverting resources into gold mining at the expense of other economic activities. A free banking system would mitigate this issue, as an increase in money demand would lead to reduced interbank clearing, increasing bank reserves and allowing them to create more money (Selgin, 1988, p. 67). Conversely, a decrease in money demand would result in a contraction of the money supply.

In summary, Mises supports the free banking system because he believes it approximates a pure gold standard with a very high reserve ratio, while Selgin defends it for its ability to adapt away from that standard (with a very low ratio of 10% in some numerical examples), facilitating adjustments that would be impossible with a 100% gold reserve.

8.1.12 Warehouse Banking (100% Reserves)

The warehouse bank system differs from the free banking model in that banks are prohibited from creating money. By law, they must fully back their deposit accounts with commodity currency reserves, resulting in 100% covered deposits. In this scenario, demand deposit banks function as mere money warehouses, holding all commodity currencies deposited by their customers. According to Rothbard's definition, such monetary institutions cannot experience inflation or deflation. The income of these banks comes primarily from fees for the warehousing and payment services they offer to customers. Following Rothbard (2005 [1962]), many economists within the Austrian School have advocated for a system of non-fractional bank reserves (e.g., Skousen, 1996 [1977]; Reisman, 1996, p. 954; Hoppe et al., 1998; Huerta de Soto, 2006 [1998]; Hülsmann 2008a).

Opponents of free banking raise several concerns, primarily regarding the stability of the monetary system under fractional reserve banking. The slightest doubt about a bank's solvency can trigger a rush of depositors seeking to withdraw their funds. The lower the reserve ratio, the smaller the fraction available for withdrawal. This anxiety can spread to other banks, leading to a contagion that results in a banking panic, potentially ruining all banks and causing severe deflation due to a sharp contraction in the money supply. Selgin and White (1996, p. 91) argue that fractional-reserve banks could have their customers sign safeguard clauses, providing them with a set period during a banking panic to gather the required gold, with compensation for customers negatively affected by the delay. However, this argument may underestimate the challenges banks would face during a panic.

For Rothbard (2008 [1983], pp. 97–99), the creation of fiduciary money is an act of fraud because it involves lending money that does not belong to the banks; it belongs to their depositors. Rothbard contends that the only difference between creating fiduciary money and counterfeiting is that the former is not illegal. Selgin and White (1996, pp. 86–92) counter this assertion by stating that if customers understand that banks are lending out their deposits, the transfer of ownership of the currency to the banks is both legal and legitimate, as it occurs by mutual consent. Huerta de Soto (2006 [1998], p. 19) criticizes Selgin and White's reasoning, highlighting significant differences between loan contracts and deposit contracts, both economically (in terms of interest payment or non-payment) and legally (involving transfer vs. custody). He argues that the fractional reserve system relies on an unacceptable conflation of these two types of contracts, as customers of fractional reserve banks are expected to both deposit and lend their money to the bank, which requires them to engage in two incompatible activities simultaneously (see also Hoppe et al., 1998).

8.1.13 A Downward Trend in Prices that Is Not Deflation in Rothbard's Sense

Under the monetary institutions proposed by the Austrian School, the price level of consumer goods would likely experience a long-term decline, in contrast to the current system where prices tend to rise. This gradual decrease in prices would be a reflection of improvements in labor productivity, akin to the price drops we observe in products like computers, flat screens, and cell phones. However, this overall reduction in consumer goods prices would not be classified as deflation, as the money supply (for instance, gold) would continue to grow slowly each year. Consequently, debtors would not face increased difficulties in repaying their debts, nor would corporate profitability rates decline, since the decrease in the unit prices of products would be more than compensated for by the growth in production (Reisman, 1996, p. 955; Selgin, 1997; for a recent and systematic defense of deflation, see Bagus, 2015).

8.2 The Austrian Business Cycle Theory (ABCT)

8.2.1 A Monetary Theory of the Business Cycle

The Austrian business cycle theory or "ABCT," commonly referred to as the "monetary" theory or more specifically, the "theory of circulation credit," was developed by Mises in the early 1910s (1980 [1912]). His framework is based on an economic system that utilizes metallic money (such as gold or silver) alongside banks that issue fiduciary money. This theory outlines a cyclical sequence of an ascending phase (the boom) that comes to an abrupt halt (the crisis), followed by a descending phase (the recession). Thus, it is more than just a theory of banking panics; although such panics, which can arise from fractional reserve banking, may accompany the crisis. This theory has been applied to significant economic downturns, including the Great Depression of the 1930s and the stagflation of the 1970s, as well as various other crises, including the more recent subprime mortgage crisis of 2006–2008.

8.2.2 The Circulation Credit

Mises distinguishes between two types of banking activities regarding credit operations:

1. *Credit negotiation*: In this scenario, banks borrow and then invest their customers' savings, profiting from the difference between the interest rate earned on these investments and the rate at which they borrow from savers.
2. *Issuing credit*: Here, banks extend credit, not from previously accumulated savings but by creating fiduciary money from their customers' deposit accounts. In this case, banks lend their depositors' money and their income consists of the interest accrued on these loans.

Mises refers to the first type as *commodity credit* and the second as *circulation credit*. When a loan based on circulation credit is repaid, the money created during that transaction is eliminated. However, the bank can quickly recreate the same amount and issue a new loan.

8.2.3 Circulation Credit and Money Interest Rate

Wicksell (1936 [1898], pp. 102–106) introduced a well-known distinction between the *natural* and the *money* rate of interest. The natural rate is the interest rate that would prevail in an economy without money, depending solely on the overall real economic conditions. In contrast, the money rate refers to the interest rates on loans in money, particularly those issued by banks. Wicksell mainly examined the effects of discrepancies between these two rates on the price level, demonstrating that if the money rate is lower than the natural rate, producers benefit from this difference. This, in turn, increases their demand for goods and services, leading to higher prices; conversely, if the money rate exceeds the natural rate, demand decreases.

Mises (1980 [1912]) adopts this distinction but approaches the question from a different angle. He assumes that banks are simultaneously increasing their circulation loans (noting that a single bank cannot significantly raise its circulation loans without suffering a substantial depletion of its reserves due to the law of adverse clearings; see Sect. 8.1.11). To place these additional loans, banks must lower the money interest rate, which then falls below the natural rate. If the issuance of circulation credit is large enough, the money rate may approach zero, although banks will not allow it to fall below a very low rate necessary to cover their operational costs associated with issuing circulation credit. Mises analyzes this process by inquiring whether there are any restorative forces that would bring the money rate back toward the natural rate (1980 [1912], pp. 398–404; 1928, pp. 118–130).

8.2.4 The Boom

The first phase of this process involves an expansion of circulation credit issued by banks and directed toward the capital market. As previously noted, the money interest rate declines. Companies that could not secure financing due to insufficient profitability in relation to the interest rate suddenly find themselves able to obtain credit because it has become more accessible. For example, a business that would earn 4% when the natural interest rate is 5% would typically not receive financing. However, if the rate drops to 3% due to the expansion of credit, the business can proceed with its plans.

The result of this expansion resembles the effects of an increase in commodity credit, causing the production structure to lengthen as if there were a genuine accumulation of capital. Economic conditions then *appear* favorable: companies have access to additional funds, which increases their demand for productive factors, especially labor. This heightened demand tends to drive up the prices of these factors. While the prices of consumer goods will also rise, this increase typically occurs with a time lag compared to the factors of production. The delay occurs because the owners of these factors (particularly workers) must first spend their increased monetary income on consumer goods before any significant price adjustments happen.

8.2.5 The Crisis

When credit expansion halts or even slows down (which is inevitable, see Sect. 8.2.8), the previously described effects are *reversed*, triggering an economic crisis.

Initially, interest rates rise again since they are no longer artificially lowered by the expansion of credit. Consequently, the profitability of many projects that were initiated to capitalize on lower interest rates and abundant credit *suddenly collapses*. The crisis is most apparent in projects launched at the higher levels of the production structure. Credit expansion has led to a lengthening of this structure, reallocating resources toward these upper stages. When credit expansion ceases, the forces favoring a shortening of the structure gain prominence.

During the boom phase, prices for production factors rose before consumer goods prices, generating profits at higher stages and attracting resources there. However, with the end of credit expansion, the consumption demand of workers once again becomes significant, driving up consumer goods prices relative to factor prices. As a result, profits begin to shift toward the lower stages of production, closer to final consumption.

The decline in profitability at the upper stages, combined with rising profitability at the lower stages, signals the onset of the crisis. In a short period, many companies at the top of the production structure are compelled to scale back or even shut down. This massive fall in the profitability of firms located in the higher stages constitutes the crisis. The lengthening of the structure that resulted from the issuance of circulation credit was artificial; it did not align with the true intertemporal preferences of economic actors. The crisis is the moment when the real economic situation becomes apparent.

8.2.6 The Recession

The recession is the painful adjustment that follows the crisis: the structure shortens and the system is restored to its intertemporal equilibrium between consumption and investment.

The boom typically lasts for several years, gradually and subtly widening the intertemporal imbalance. The full extent of this misalignment is abruptly revealed in the crisis. While shorter than the boom, the recovery period may still take 1 or 2 years. However, the end of a recession can be delayed by counterproductive government actions, such as keeping wages high, preventing layoffs, subsidizing struggling sectors, imposing protectionist measures, or doubling down on money creation.

In a recession, some specific production factors created during the boom lose value, resulting in significant capital losses. Other specific factors, better suited to a sustainable balance between consumption and investment, must be produced in larger quantities and combined with labor that is being reallocated across stages. Beyond labor, other convertible resources will need to be transferred to different branches or firms. Correcting the extensive business errors made during the boom requires time and relies on the market's trial-and-error process. The temporary impoverishment brought on by the recession is unavoidable.

8.2.7 The Secondary Deflation

When the crisis hits, economic actors quickly realize they need to act with much greater caution. Banks restrict lending, finding it too risky in a now volatile and unpredictable economic environment. Worse, some banks may face bankruptcy if borrowers default on loans, potentially leading to a chain of bank failures and a reduction in the supply of fiduciary money.

Additionally, firms and households become more anxious about the future and tend to increase their demand for cash, seeking to hold larger reserves in case their personal situations worsen. If money supply contracts and prices begin to fall, people may delay purchases, expecting even lower prices. This waiting behavior further reduces demand for goods, reinforcing the deflationary trend.

This "secondary deflation" is widely considered harmful by most economists, but Rothbard offers a different view, seeing its effects as "beneficial" (1983 [1963], pp. 22–25). He argues that increased cash reserves are desired by individuals, and the resulting rise in money's purchasing power aligns with their need for liquidity in uncertain times. The accompanying reduction in consumption is actually favorable, helping to rebalance the relationship between consumption and investment. Moreover, falling prices do not obstruct economic recovery, as firms focus on maintaining the margin between revenue and costs rather than absolute price levels. Ultimately, this secondary deflation is only temporary; at some point, stability returns, and spending picks up again.

8.2.8 *Can the Boom Last Indefinitely?*

Could banks, by rapidly increasing the issuance of circulation credit, delay the onset of a crisis and the necessary rebalancing of the economic system? Is it feasible for them to prolong the boom without ever having to end it? Mises and his successors argue that the answer is no. Accelerated credit expansion inevitably leads to hyperinflation, destroying money. There are only two potential outcomes:

- The first is a *readjustment crisis*, which occurs when banks cease or even just slow down the expansion of credit. This may happen if banks are compelled to restrict their credit expansion due to a low metal reserve ratio (for their convertibility on-demand operations or in compliance with government regulations).
- The second outcome is *hyperinflation* and the eventual destruction of the currency if banks continue to expand credit without restraint.

Ultimately, there is indeed a restoring force that drives the interest rate back to its "natural" level after the expansion of circulation credit has caused it to diverge. Not even the rush into hyperinflation can prevent the return to the "natural" rate once money has been destroyed.

8.2.9 *Illustrating the Cycle with Hayekian Triangles*

Hayek's (1931) and Rothbard's (1962, pp. 850–877) analyses are aligned with Mises'. They begin by distinguishing between simple economic fluctuations and the business cycle itself. Typical economic shocks lead to simple fluctuations: these shocks initiate processes that guide the system toward a new equilibrium, as seen with demand shocks, technical shocks, resource shocks (see Sect. 3.2.13), and intertemporal preference shocks (which result in capital accumulation: see Sect. 5.2.7).

In contrast, credit expansion generates a business cycle characterized by a boom phase that moves the system *away from equilibrium*. The influx of new liquidity into the capital market causes *malinvestment*, which is marked by overinvestment in higher stages of production and underinvestment in lower stages, resulting in a misallocation of resources away from final consumption. The balance between consumption and investment, which economic actors seek based on their intertemporal preferences, is disrupted by credit expansion, which increases investment spending more than consumption spending. This imbalance not only lengthens the production period (stretching the production structure) but also expands it horizontally (monetarily) due to the increase in the quantity of money, as illustrated in Fig. 8.1.

When economic agents, such as factor owners and capitalists, receive their income, they allocate their spending between consumption and investment based on their time preferences. However, a *new injection of liquidity*, if substantial enough, can disrupt the rebalancing between consumption and investment once more. This can sustain or even extend the artificially lengthened structure. This process can continue with further injections of liquidity, leading to successive disruptions (see Fig. 8.2).

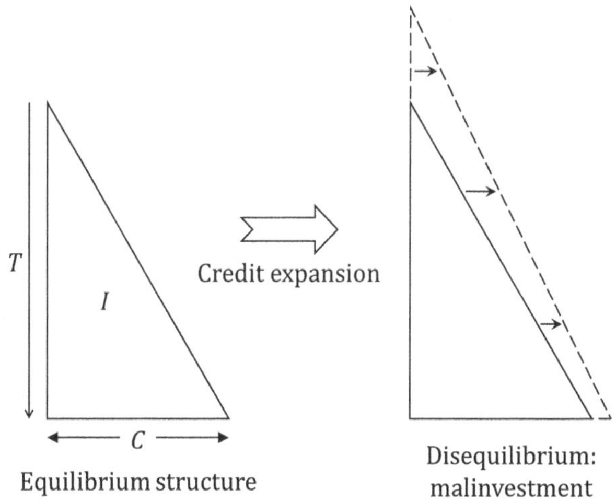

Fig. 8.1 Credit expansion leads to malinvestment: the base of the Hayekian triangle *C* represents annual monetary expenditure on consumer goods, the height *T* represents total production time, and the area *I* total investment

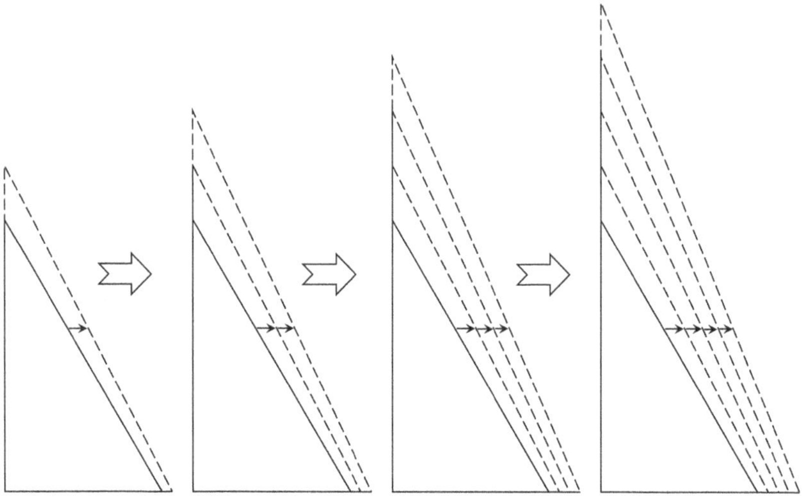

Fig. 8.2 The boom: successive injections of credit increasingly distort and unbalance the production structure

However, unless exponential inflation ultimately destroys money, there comes a point when credit expansion slows and is no longer sufficient to override the intertemporal choices made by economic agents. At that moment, they re-establish their desired balance between consumption and investment, causing the interest rate to rise toward its equilibrium value (which may have shifted due to the redistribution effects of inflation). This readjustment of the production structure to get back in line with intertemporal preferences constitutes the crisis and recession, which are more severe if the boom phase is longer and the imbalance between consumption and investment is more exacerbated (see Fig. 8.3).

8.2.10 Two Metaphors

Mises illustrates his cycle theory using the metaphor of a construction site (1946, p. 223). During the boom phase, it is akin to an overly ambitious construction project being launched. Available resources are utilized to dig foundations and erect the initial walls and pillars. However, as the project progresses, the builders realize they have been overconfident and lack the necessary resources to complete the construction. This realization

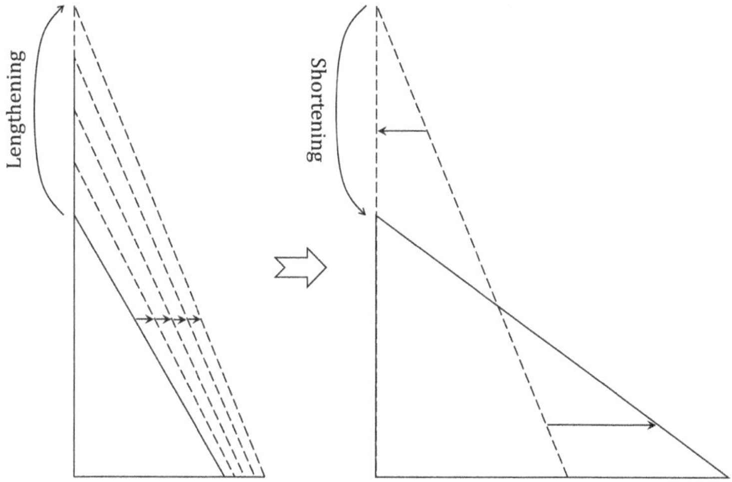

Fig. 8.3 The recession: when credit expansion ceases or slows, the production structure adjusts back to the intertemporal equilibrium between consumption and investment

marks the crisis phase. Some of the resources invested in the initial construction are wasted, and ultimately, they must settle for a more modest structure—a less complex production framework.

Rothbard (1962, p. 861) employs a different metaphor. He likens the succession of boom and crisis to drunkenness (the euphoria of the boom), followed by sobering up (the "hangover" of the recession), or to drug addiction followed by painful detoxification. This analogy highlights how the Austrian interpretation of the cycle inverts common perceptions: while the boom phase appears favorable and beneficial, it is actually when the system becomes ill, whereas the recession phase represents a period of recovery or rehabilitation.

8.2.11 Business Cycle and Price Level

In Mises' theory, the cycle is accompanied by rising prices during the boom phase, with production factor prices increasing more rapidly than consumer goods prices. This occurs because the issuance of additional circulation credit raises the overall quantity of money, leading to an increase in the price level. However, in a specific historical context, this tendency to raise prices can be countered by forces that lower the price level, such as increases in production (Hayek, 1966 [1929]; Rothbard, 1962, p. 862). As a result, the imbalance that eventually triggers the crisis can grow even while the price level remains stable, as was observed in the years leading up to the 1929 crisis.

During the recession phase, prices for consumer goods tend to rise faster than those for production factors. Prices may also decline if deflation—a contraction in the money supply—occurs, often due to a banking panic that leads to the bankruptcy of certain banks and the destruction of a portion of the fiduciary money. This phenomenon is particularly associated with the fractional reserve system in the case of metallic money. In contrast, with state-issued scriptural money, money creation may continue during the crisis, potentially resulting in stagflation, as seen in the 1970s when economic depression coincided with significant price increases.

An important aspect to note is that Austrian cycle theory does not assign a causal role to price-level variations, as it emphasizes the *relative prices* of consumer goods and production factors (Hayek, 1966 [1929], pp. 103–105).

8.2.12 Fighting the Crisis?

For Austrian economists, a crisis is not an illness but a healing phase that restores the economic system to the intertemporal equilibrium desired by economic agents. Therefore, ***the government should refrain from interfering with this readjustment process***: the crisis should not be fought. Consequently, the political options are quite limited. By imposing higher taxes on workers to benefit capitalists, the government could, in theory, increase savings and investment, thereby cushioning the impact of the crisis while justifying some of the investments that had artificially lengthened the production structure in the first place. However, no Austrian economist advocates for such a policy.

The most significant error would be for the government to accelerate credit expansion and further lower interest rates. This would only perpetuate the intertemporal imbalance in the production structure and prolong the depression. This inflationary policy, which Austrians reject, is precisely what was implemented in the United States to combat the depression resulting from the 2007 subprime crisis. Here, the opposition to Keynesian remedies is direct: what is seen as a solution to the crisis from a Keynesian perspective is viewed by Austrians as a factor that exacerbates the situation.

8.2.13 Avoiding the Cycle

In the long term, the best way to address a crisis is to prevent the business cycle from occurring in the first place. According to Rothbard (1962, p. 862), using gold as money with non-fractional bank reserves would offer complete protection against the cycle, whereas state-issued (fiat) scriptural money is most conducive to credit expansion and thus to the cycle. Mises argues that even within a free banking system (metallic money with fractional reserves), the experiences of past crises would lead banks concerned about the reputation of their fiduciary money to exercise caution in issuing circulation credit. However, government interference—such as establishing a privileged central bank and suspending the requirement for banks to convert notes and deposits into metal money on demand during crises (and today, we might add: deposit guarantees)—has consistently aimed at promoting and facilitating credit expansion by alleviating banks of their responsibilities. In Mises' view, the "ultimate cause" is ***ideological***: cycles will persist as long as people erroneously believe that lower interest rates achieved through credit expansion can create widespread and lasting prosperity (Mises, 1928, pp. 139–141).

8.2.14 The Great Depression in the United States (1929–1941)

Austrian economists offer an interpretation of the Great Depression that stands in stark contrast to the commonly accepted narrative (Mises, 1931; Rothbard, 1983 [1963]; Murphy, 2009).

According to the conventional account, the capitalist system experienced one of its periodic crises in 1929 due to its inherent instability, which stemmed from the irrational exuberance of entrepreneurs and investors. US President Herbert Hoover's policies were seen as timid and insufficiently interventionist, leading the system into a deep depression with unemployment reaching unprecedented levels, peaking at 25% in 1933. Fortunately, President Franklin Roosevelt, elected in 1932, implemented a robust, proactive economic policy that ultimately resolved the crisis and "saved capitalism from itself."

The Austrian interpretation challenges this "canonical" narrative at every turn. They argue that the credit expansion of the 1920s, which was encouraged by the Federal Reserve, insidiously destabilized the economic system. This imbalance went unnoticed because the price level remained stable during this period; the upward pressure on prices from credit expansion was offset by downward pressure from strong economic growth. When the crisis was ignited by the stock market crash in October 1929, President Hoover adopted an interventionist approach that would later characterize the New Deal. His policies included maintaining wage levels, expanding credit, investing in public works, reinforcing protectionism, increasing the public deficit, restricting immigration, and raising taxes. However, the maintenance of nominal wages amid significant deflation from 1931 to 1933 resulted in rising real wages, which in turn caused unemployment to surge. Despite 3 years of unprecedented political activism aimed at combating the economic crisis, conditions only worsened, and the depression deepened significantly. According to Austrian economists, this *political activism* obstructed the necessary rebalancing and significantly prolonged the downturn.

Franklin D. Roosevelt was elected president in 1932 on a platform that promised to reduce government interference in the economy. However, upon taking office in March 1933, he continued and intensified the policies of his predecessor, yielding little success in alleviating the Great Depression, with the unemployment rate still exceeding 17% in 1939.

As for the elimination of unemployment during World War II, Austrians argue that this was not the result of massive public spending on the war effort, but rather due to a substantial increase in private savings (Skousen, 1996) and a relative decline in real wages (where real wages rose at a slower rate than labor productivity: Vedder & Gallaway, 1997 [1993], pp. 152–157). The Austrian interpretation of the causes, nature, trajectory, and resolution of the Great Depression contrasts sharply with the mainstream viewpoint.

8.2.15 *The Stagflation of the 1970s*

While the sources of the economic imbalance in the 1920s were obscured by price-level stability, the origins of the stagflation—a combination of stagnation and inflation—of the 1970s were starkly apparent. In the two decades following World War II, governments implemented inflationary policies to "stimulate demand" and address unemployment. As early as 1950, Hayek cautioned that these "Keynesian" policies were likely to lead to increasingly expansive monetary policies that would become progressively less effective in combating unemployment (1967 [1950], p. 271).

Indeed, when a government adopts such policies, it may temporarily preserve jobs that would otherwise be lost, but this preservation relies on monetary manipulation that gives these jobs an illusory sense of profitability. Maintaining these positions necessitates ever-increasing amounts of inflation to prevent the adjustments that would cause them to disappear. This creates a challenging situation: halting or even just slowing the creation of money would result in significant job losses. However, inflation negatively impacts the productive efficiency of the economic system (see Sect. 8.1.6), as demonstrated during the 1970s.

When it appeared that the high levels of inflation in this period not only failed to reduce unemployment but also slowed down economic growth, the US government decided in 1979 to combat stagflation by restricting money creation. Annual inflation peaked at 13.5% in 1980, subsequently declining to around 3–4% from 1983 onward. However, this shift was accompanied by two successive recessions, from June to July 1980 and from July 1981 to November 1982 (source: National Bureau of Economic Research). Unemployment soared to its highest levels since the Great Depression, exceeding 10% from September 1982 to June 1983 (source: U.S. Department of Labor). While the "Keynesian" inflationary policies of the post-war period initially alleviated rising unemployment, in the long term, they ultimately contributed to the economic downturn of the 1970s (Hayek, 1978, pp. 191–231), from which the United States only emerged at the cost of record unemployment in the early 1980s.

8.2.16 The Subprime Crisis and the Great Recession (2006–2008)

For Austrian economists, the "subprime crisis," which began in the United States in 2007, serves as a textbook example of their theory.

Between 2001 and 2003, the Federal Reserve implemented an aggressive monetary policy to lift the United States out of the recession that followed the collapse of the dot-com bubble in March 2000 and the September 11 terrorist attacks. During this period, it reduced the federal funds rate from over 6% in early 2001 to just 1% by June 2003 (Thornton, 2008). This was achieved through an "open market" policy that involved creating and injecting significant amounts of reserve money into the economy, which were then multiplied by banks (Murphy, 2007). The large quantities of money generated were directed into the capital market (credit expansion) at increasingly low interest rates, often reaching borrowers with high risk. The drop in interest rates also encouraged long-term borrowing, particularly in the real estate sector, where 30-year mortgage rates hit record lows in the first half of 2003 (Thornton, 2008).

From 2004 until mid-2006, the Federal Reserve raised interest rates due to concerns about a resurgence of inflation. However, this tightening of credit starved the real estate market of the funds necessary to sustain demand, leading to a decrease in home sales prices. Consequently, not only did many variable-rate borrowers struggle to meet their mortgage payments due to rising interest rates, but lending institutions were also left with homes that had insufficient value as collateral. This accumulation of non-repayable mortgages represented a significant malinvestment—a substantial amount of capital squandered during the credit expansion phase of 2001–2003. The profitability of the real estate market had been artificially maintained by money creation and vanished along with it. The ensuing correction resulted in the bankruptcy of numerous financial institutions and, under normal circumstances, would have led to deflation as the money issued by these bankrupt banks disappeared. However, given the strong inflationary stimulus policies enacted by various central banks, deflation was avoided.

Austrians have provided extensive commentary online and several publications examining the various facets of this "subprime" cycle. The real estate bubble was quickly identified (Shostak, 2003) and analyzed (Thornton, 2006). Authors such as Huerta de Soto (2008), Rallo (2009), Horwitz (2009), Woods (2009), Salerno (2012), and Fillieule (2013) have demonstrated the relevance of Austrian theory in understanding this crisis. Reisman (2008) highlighted the role of monetary authorities in triggering the cycle, while Hülsmann (2008b) emphasized the moral hazard posed by central banks to the banking system, where lenders are encouraged to take reckless risks, knowing that the central bank will bail them out in times of trouble.

References

Bagus, P. (2015). *In Defense of Deflation*. Springer.

Fillieule, R. (2013). The Explanation of the Subprime Crisis According to the Austrian School: A Defense and Illustration. *Journal des Économistes et des Études Humaines, 19*(1), 101–136.

Hayek, F. A. (1931). *Prices and Production*. George Routledge and Sons.

Hayek, F. A. (1939 [1932]). A Note on the Development of the Doctrine of "Forced Saving". In F. A. Hayek (Ed.), *Profits, Interest and Investment, and*

Other Essays on the Theory of Industrial Fluctuations (pp. 183–197). George Routledge & Sons.

Hayek, F. A. (1966 [1929]). *Monetary Theory and the Trade Cycle.* Augustus M. Kelley.

Hayek, F. A. (1967 [1950]). Full Employment, Planning and Inflation. In F. A. Hayek (Ed.), *Studies in Philosophy, Politics and Economics* (pp. 270–279). Routledge & Kegan Paul.

Hayek, F. A. (1978). *New Studies in Philosophy, Politics, Economics and the History of Ideas.* Routledge & Kegan Paul.

Hayek, F. A. (1990 [1976]). *Denationalisation of Money: The Argument Refined. An Analysis of the Theory and Practice of Concurrent Currencies.* The Institute of Economic Affairs.

Hazlitt, H. (1978). *The Inflation Crisis, and How to Resolve It.* Arlington House.

Hoppe, H.-H., Hülsmann, J. G., & Block, W. (1998). Against Fiduciary Media. *Quarterly Journal of Austrian Economics, 1*(1), 19–50.

Horwitz, S. (2000). *Microfoundations and Macroeconomics. An Austrian Perspective.* Routledge.

Horwitz, S. (2009). *The Microeconomic Foundations of Macroeconomic Disorder: An Austrian Perspective on the Great Recession of 2008* (p. 23). Working Paper, Mercatus Center, George Mason University.

Huerta de Soto, J. (2006 [1998]). *Money, Bank Credit, and Economic Cycles.* Ludwig von Mises Institute.

Huerta de Soto, J. (2008, October 6). Financial Crisis and Recession. *Mises Daily.*

Hülsmann, J. G. (2006). The Political Economy of Moral Hazard. *Politická Ekonomie, 1*, 35–47.

Hülsmann, J. G. (2008a). *The Ethics of Money Production.* Ludwig von Mises Institute.

Hülsmann, J. G. (2008b, June 3). Beware the Moral Hazard Trivializers. *Mises Daily.*

Murphy, R. P. (2007, October 1). The Worst Recession in 25 Years? *Mises Daily.*

Murphy, R. P. (2009). *The Politically Incorrect Guide to the Great Depression and the New Deal.* Regnery.

Rallo, J. R. (2009, January 6). Economic Crisis and Paradigm Shift. *Mises Daily.*

Reisman, G. (1996). *Capitalism. A Treatise on Economics.* Jameson Books.

Reisman, G. (2008, October 23). The Myth that Laissez Faire Is Responsible for Our Present Crisis. *Mises Daily.*

Rothbard, M. N. (1962). *Man, Economy, and State. A Treatise on Economic Principles.* D. Van Nostrand.

Rothbard, M. N. (1977 [1970]). *Power and Market. Government and the Economy.* Sheed Andrews and McMeel.

Rothbard, M. N. (1983 [1963]). *America's Great Depression.* Richardson & Snyder.

Rothbard, M. N. (1988). The Myth of Free Banking in Scotland. *Review of Austrian Economics, 2*(1), 229–245.

Rothbard, M. N. (1990 [1963]). *What Has Government Done to Our Money?* Ludwig von Mises Institute.
Rothbard, M. N. (2005 [1962]). *The Case for a 100 Percent Gold Dollar.* Ludwig von Mises Institute.
Rothbard, M. N. (2008 [1983]). *The Mystery of Banking.* Ludwig von Mises Institute.
Salerno, J. T. (1993). Mises and Hayek Dehomogenized. *Review of Austrian Economics, 6*(2), 113–146.
Salerno, J. T. (2012). A Reformulation of Austrian Business Cycle Theory in Light of the Financial Crisis. *Quarterly Journal of Austrian Economics, 15*(1), 3–44.
Selgin, G. (1988). *The Theory of Free Banking. Money Supply Under Competitive Note Issue.* Rowman & Littlefield Publishers.
Selgin, G. (1997). *Less than Zero. The Case for a Falling Price Level in a Growing Economy.* Institute of Economic Affairs.
Selgin, G., & White, L. H. (1996). In Defense of Fiduciary Media-or, We are *Not* Devo(lutionists), We are Misesians! *Review of Austrian Economics, 9*(2), 83–107.
Sennholz, H. F. (1977). *Age of Inflation.* Western Islands.
Shostak, F. (2003, March 4). Housing Bubble: Myth or Reality? *Mises Daily.*
Skousen, M. (1996 [1977]). *Economics of a Pure Gold Standard.* The Foundation for Economic Education.
Thornton, M. (2006, June 12). The Economics of Housing Bubbles. *Mises Institute Working Paper.*
Thornton, M. (2008, September 27). The Housing Bubble in Four Easy Steps. *Mises Daily.*
Vedder, R. K., & Gallaway, L. E. (1997 [1993]). *Out of Work. Unemployment and Government in Twentieth-Century America.* New York University Press.
Von Mises, L. (1928). Monetary Stabilization and Cyclical Policy. In L. von Mises (1978) (pp. 57–171).
Von Mises, L. (1931). The Causes of the Economic Crisis. In L. von Mises (1978) (pp. 173–203).
Von Mises, L. (1946). The Trade Cycle and Credit Expansion: The Economic Consequences of Cheap Money. In L. von Mises (1978) (pp. 215–226).
Von Mises, L. (1978). *On the Manipulation of Money and Credit.* Free Market Books.
Von Mises, L. (1980 [1912]). *The Theory of Money and Credit.* LibertyClassics.
Von Mises, L. (1998 [1949]). *Human Action. A Treatise on Economics.* Ludwig von Mises Institute.
Wicksell, K. (1936 [1898]). *Interest and Prices. A Study of the Causes Regulating the Value of Money.* Macmillan.
Woods, T. E. (2009). *Meltdown. A Free-Market Look at Why the Stock Market Collapsed, the Economy Tanked, and Government Bailouts Will Make Things Worse.* Regnery.

CHAPTER 9

State and Market

Abstract Interventionism consists in government actions that distort market processes, such as price controls, production regulations, and monopoly privileges. Austrian economists contend that interventionism impoverishes society by causing adverse unintended consequences that necessitate further interventions, which, in turn, lead to additional negative effects. The chapter then reviews different types of taxes and their impacts. Finally, it highlights Mises' critique of collectivism, emphasizing the impossibility of economic calculation without market prices and private property, and Hayek's critique, which focuses rather on the overwhelming complexity and knowledge dispersion that a collectivist state cannot effectively manage. Ultimately, Austrian economists attribute inflation, crises, mass unemployment, and monopolistic restrictions to state intervention rather than market processes.

Keywords Price control • Regulation • Monopoly privilege • Taxes • Collectivism

In the 1920s, Mises (1981 [1922], Chap. 34, 1996 [1929]) developed a clear and uncompromising theory on state interventionism, critiquing government interference in the market. According to Mises, when the

R. Fillieule, *The Austrian School of Economics*, Palgrave Studies in Austrian Economics,
https://doi.org/10.1007/978-3-031-83414-1_9

State intervenes—whether through price controls, production regulations, wealth redistribution, or by injecting money into the economy via the central bank—it ultimately impoverishes society, lowering the average standard of living. Such interventions, he argued, may be justified based on value judgments favoring redistribution from the majority to specific minority groups, but they cannot be defended as ways to enrich society as a whole. Influenced by Mises' anti-interventionist stance, most later Austrian School economists adopted liberal views. While some of his followers, like Rothbard (1998 [1982]), embraced a form of pro-capitalist anarchism, others, such as Hayek (1944), supported a certain degree of state involvement in the market.

9.1 Interventionism

9.1.1 Capitalism, Collectivism, and Interventionism

Mises (1998a [1940]) identifies three main types of economic systems:

1. *Capitalism*, or the "unhampered" market economy, is defined by private ownership of the means of production, with the state's role limited to protecting "the life, health, and private property of its citizens against force and fraud" (1998a [1940], p. 8).
2. *Collectivism*, or socialism, is defined as public ownership of the material means of production.
3. *Interventionism* differs from collectivism in that it does not seek to eliminate private ownership of production factors and from capitalism in that it seeks to restrict the scope of actions available to those who own these factors.

Governments implement interventionism to improve the well-being of the governed. The central question, which Mises (1926, p. 17) calls *the problem of interventionism*, is whether interventionist policies can achieve this goal in the long term. His answer is no: interventionist policies ultimately lower the average standard of living, all else being equal, even though they may benefit certain segments of the population in the short term.

9.1.2 The Concept of Intervention

Mises argues that governmental intervention in the market occurs when authorities force the owners of productive resources to use these resources "in a different manner than they otherwise would" (Mises, 1926, p. 4). According to this view, there are two main forms of intervention:

1. *Price controls* (e.g., minimum wage laws)
2. *Production controls* (e.g., legal prohibitions on the production of certain goods)

In the Misesian perspective, government measures designed to protect private property do not constitute intervention. Likewise, nationalization and state redistribution are not considered interventions, as they do not disrupt the market process itself. However, Rothbard (1977 [1970]) and Lavoie (1982) support a broader view of intervention that includes nationalized enterprises, as well as government taxation and spending, offering a potentially more comprehensive definition of economic intervention.

9.1.3 Price Controls

Mises (1923) considers price controls—legal restrictions that prevent sellers from setting prices above or below a certain level—as a key example of government intervention in the market.

Imagine a government aiming to raise the standard of living for its most disadvantaged populations. To achieve this, it sets a price ceiling on a basic good, capping the maximum price it can be sold for—similar to how French revolutionaries capped grain prices in 1793. This administratively lowered price is intended to bring basic foodstuff within the reach of the poorest, but it leads to *rationing*: demand for the good exceeds the available supply, as more buyers want to purchase the good at the reduced price, while fewer sellers are willing to sell (some sellers may even keep their stock for personal use).

Not all buyers will be able to obtain the good. Sellers may respond by serving customers on a "first come, first served" basis, causing long queues and wasted time for buyers. Alternatively, they may turn to black-market sales or demand kickbacks, where prices rise significantly to account for the legal risks involved. Sellers may also favor specific buyers, such as family, friends, loyal customers, or members of their ethnic group. In response, the government might impose stricter penalties to deter black-market activities or implement a distribution system to ensure at least partial access for everyone.

However, more significant issues arise over time. The reduction in price decreases the profitability of producing the good, causing producers to lower their production levels. To sustain price controls, the government would need to incentivize production by reducing the prices of input factors such as natural resources and capital goods. This pattern of price control would then gradually extend across the economic system, ultimately leading to comprehensive state control or "complete socialization of production" (Mises, 1923, p. 102).

9.1.4 *From Selective to Universal Price Control*

Selective price control, limited to only a few goods, can lead consumers to shift their spending toward substitute goods (Rothbard, 1977 [1970], p. 26). This increase in demand for substitutes drives up their prices, raises their profitability, and attracts capital to expand production in these areas. As a result, the production structure becomes distorted, with fewer controlled goods and more substitutes than consumers might prefer. This distortion is typically unintended by the government, which then faces a choice:

- It can lift price controls, which would reverse the distortion and realign production with consumer preferences.
- Or it can expand price controls to the input costs of production, and eventually to all levels of production factors until *every* price in the economy is controlled.

In the latter scenario, price control becomes *universal*. With all prices controlled, consumers can no longer shift spending to substitutes, effectively "anesthetizing" part of their money, as Rothbard describes it: since rationing has spread everywhere, there are not enough goods to spend money on. Queuing and black-market transactions become commonplace.

9.1.5 *The Minimum Wage*

While a maximum price (price ceiling) generally leads to rationing, a minimum price (price floor) creates *surpluses* because the quantity demanded at this price is lower than the quantity sellers are willing to supply. The minimum wage is a classic example (Mises, 1923, pp. 103–105).

If a minimum wage is implemented *only in unionized sectors*, production costs rise in these sectors, lowering the rate of return, as workers now cost more (due to the minimum wage) than the value they produce (their discounted marginal productivity). Capital tends to flow into uncontrolled (non-unionized) sectors, where returns remain higher. The reduction in investment in the controlled sectors decreases supply and raises prices (eventually returning the rate of return to equilibrium), but it also leads to layoffs or fewer hirings. Surplus workers will then seek employment in uncontrolled sectors, increasing labor supply and driving wages down in those sectors (although wage declines are partially offset by the influx of capital into these sectors). Consequently, wage increases in controlled industries ultimately result in wage declines in uncontrolled industries and disrupt the production structure initially determined by consumer demand. To prevent layoffs in controlled (unionized) industries, the government must then intervene further.

If a minimum wage applies *across all branches*, the quantity of labor supplied exceeds demand. The resulting surplus of workers cannot find employment in other sectors, as all are subject to controls, leading to "institutional unemployment" that is a "permanent mass phenomenon" (Mises, 1998c [1949], pp. 763–764). Reduced employment diminishes production, lowering the average standard of living. The minimum wage primarily impacts low-skilled labor, further distorting production by disproportionately affecting industries that rely more heavily on this type of labor.

If the government mandates a minimum wage across the economy and simultaneously prohibits layoffs, nominal wages rise at the expense of returns on capital. Lower returns discourage saving and investment, prompting capital consumption and weakening productive capacity, which ultimately reduces the average standard of living. Additionally, artificially higher wages cut into entrepreneurial profits, slowing or even halting productive adaptations.

However, the government can dissolve real wage increases through inflation. A sufficient increase in the money supply raises prices, lowering the real value of the nominal wage floor and eliminating involuntary unemployment. According to Hayek (1967 [1959], p. 282), this helps explain the inflationary policies of the twentieth century: when unions managed to secure widespread wage increases, governments increased the money supply to counterbalance these rises and prevent mass unemployment.

Austrian economists argue that sustainable increases in real wages cannot be achieved through government or union intervention; only capital accumulation, technological advancement, and the intensification of labor division can accomplish this.

9.1.6 *Prohibition*

The most straightforward form of state control over production is prohibition, which involves a complete ban on producing a particular good or using a certain production method. A well-known example is the US prohibition of alcohol from 1920 to 1933. Rothbard (1977 [1970], p. 34) examines such prohibitions without making moral judgments about the goods being restricted. He concludes that prohibitions primarily harm consumers, who lose access to a desired good, except on the black market. However, black-market prices are significantly higher due to the risk premiums demanded by illegal producers and the inefficiencies resulting from the inability to mass-produce and distribute (Thornton, 1991). According to Rothbard, the only real beneficiaries of prohibition are the government agents employed to enforce the ban.

9.1.7 *Monopoly or Quasi-Monopoly Privileges*

The second form of production control involves granting a monopoly privilege, where the government allows production but limits the number of entities authorized to participate. If only one producer is permitted, this creates a monopoly; if multiple producers are allowed but with restricted competition, it forms a "quasi-monopoly." The effects are similar to prohibition but less extreme. Consumers are disadvantaged because the restricted production results in fewer goods than they would prefer. Additionally, potential producers who are barred from entering this market must shift to other industries, often accepting lower returns. This intervention distorts the structure of production, much like prohibition and price controls. The beneficiaries are the privileged producers and government officials responsible for designing and enforcing these regulations.

If demand for the monopolized good is inelastic, the monopoly can set a "monopoly price" higher than what would prevail in a competitive market, creating a profit differential known as the monopoly gain, which arises from the government-granted privilege (see Sect. 4.1.4). Should the government attempt to limit these gains by capping the monopolist's rate of return, the monopolist can easily raise operational costs rather than lower prices. When a quasi-monopoly is granted over an original factor, such as labor or natural resources, the supply of this factor tends to decrease, benefiting owners who can charge a "restrictionist" price (a result of governmental restrictions) that exceeds the price in an unrestricted market.

9.1.8 Types of State Monopolies and Quasi-Monopolies

Mises (1998b [1944]) identifies several types of state-created monopolies and quasi-monopolies, including:

- *Licenses*: Special permits required to sell certain goods or services, such as cab services and medicines.
- *Intellectual property laws*: Protections like trademarks, copyrights, and patents (discussed further below).
- *National cartels protected by tariffs*: Domestic cartels shielded from foreign competition through import taxes.
- *International cartels*: Examples include organizations like OPEC.
- *Competition restrictions*: Measures aimed at protecting small retailers from large stores or local vendors from mail-order or online competitors.

Rothbard (1977 [1970], pp. 41–80) expands this list with additional types of state-imposed restrictions, including:

- *Quality and safety standards*: While Mises views state certifications (e.g., medical degrees) as legitimate protections against fraud, Rothbard argues they act as monopolistic barriers, preventing consumers from accessing potentially more affordable medical services or alternative medicines not state-approved.
- *Immigration restrictions*: Laws that create a quasi-monopoly on labor within a country's borders.
- *Child labor laws and compulsory schooling*: These confer a quasi-monopoly on adult workers or those past compulsory schooling age.
- *Conscription*: Military drafts that remove adult workers from the labor force.

- *Minimum wage and unemployment benefits*: These policies keep some of the lowest-productivity workers out of the labor market.
- *Anti-trust laws* are discussed in the following section.
- *Conservation laws*: These restrict the exploitation of non-renewable resources, granting a virtual monopoly to those who control the limited accessible resources. In cases where governments designate extensive public lands as protected natural parks (as in the United States), land scarcity is artificially increased, driving up prices for land available for productive use and development.

9.1.9 Anti-trust Laws

Anti-trust laws aim to protect consumers from potential abuses by very large companies. Mises (1981 [1922], p. 326) notes that discussions around trusts often reflect emotional concerns, even among economists, who fear the growing monopoly power of large organizations. He acknowledges that monopolies or cartels facing inelastic demand may restrict production and raise prices, disadvantaging consumers. However, he argues this situation only rarely arises, typically when a natural resource is monopolized, as with diamonds in his era or oil today (1998c [1949], p. 368). Mises contends that, in a free market, there is no inherent tendency for monopoly prices to proliferate; rather, they tend to become rare (see Sect. 4.1.8). Thus, the original justification for anti-trust laws, such as the "restraint of trade" principle in the Sherman Act of 1890, is ultimately unconvincing. This view is further supported by historical evidence, such as the 1909 anti-trust case against Standard Oil, which was producing ever-greater quantities of oil at decreasing prices—indicating no restrictive practices (Armentano, 1996 [1982], p. 67).

Rothbard (1977 [1970], p. 60) critiques additional arguments that underpin anti-trust laws.

First argument: *large or few firms reduce competition*. This argument assumes competition can be quantified. However, Rothbard asserts that competition is a dynamic process, not a fixed quantity, where the number or size of firms is irrelevant. An industry with only one or a few large firms can still be competitive—as was the case with Standard Oil in the early twentieth century, or today's microprocessor and flat-screen producers. Reisman (1996, p. 376) adds that the large size of firms in certain industries reflects a well-functioning competitive process, where significant capital is required to achieve the efficiencies necessary to compete effectively.

Second argument: *cartels are anti-competitive*. Cartels consolidate productive resources under unified management, similar to forming a single company. By opposing cartels, anti-trust laws contradict the very concept of business formation, which also involves pooling resources and centralized management.

Third argument: *large firms can engage in predatory pricing*. Some argue a powerful company might engage in "predatory pricing" by increasing production and lowering prices to drive smaller competitors out, and then raising prices after eliminating competition. However, this scenario is highly unlikely because it requires an inelastic demand and imposes significant costs on the large firm. Smaller competitors could choose to operate minimally until the larger firm exhausts its resources. Even if a firm succeeds in monopolizing a market, the threat of new entrants would discourage it from excessively raising prices. Instead, it would aim to keep prices at a level that deters competitors, offering only a reasonable margin (Rothbard, 1962, p. 600).

From the Austrian perspective, anti-trust laws are based on flawed competition models, leading to ineffective or even harmful policy outcomes (Armentano, 1996 [1982]). The "perfect competition" model (see Sect. 4.2.8) and the structuralist "structure-conduct-performance" approach in industrial organization theory reflect a *static* view of competition. These models, implicitly or explicitly used in anti-trust legislation, fail to account for the dynamic nature of real-world competition. Many phenomena that appear inefficient in static models are, in fact, signs of an active competitive process from a dynamic perspective. For example, market concentration correlating with profitability can indicate that more efficient companies are outcompeting less profitable ones. In attempting to correct such perceived inefficiencies, anti-trust laws and broader competition policies may inadvertently penalize more successful firms. Rothbard and Armentano conclude, somewhat provocatively, that anti-trust laws can actually have anti-competitive effects: they protect less efficient producers from their more efficient rivals, effectively establishing a quasi-monopoly in favor of the former and against the latter.

9.1.10 Intellectual Property

Intellectual property laws encompass four categories: trademarks®, copyrights©, patents, and trade secrets (Kinsella, 2008 [2001]). This discussion will focus on the first three. A key question is whether these laws represent state intervention in the market or are essential components of the private property rights system characteristic of a free market economy. Scholars from the Austrian School have varied widely in their responses to this question. On one end of the spectrum, Mises (1998c [1949], p. 366) regards intellectual property in its various forms as a monopolistic privilege granted by the State. Conversely, Reisman (1996, p. 389) views it as an integral aspect of a purely capitalist system; he argues that patents encourage productive invention, leading to increased production and lower prices rather than functioning as a restrictive government monopoly.

While Mises perceives intellectual property laws—trademarks, copyrights, and patents—as monopolistic licenses, he refrains from commenting on their validity. He notes that these laws can favor certain inventions and artistic creations but also enable inventors or intellectual property holders to charge monopoly prices. Thus, he finds it challenging to justify or condemn these laws from a strictly scientific standpoint, simply stating that they raise complex issues regarding the definition and extension of property rights (1998c [1949], p. 658).

Rothbard (1962, p. 592) distinguishes trademarks from state monopolies, asserting that an individual's or company's name defines its identity and constitutes private property. By protecting the use of a name or trademark, the state is not hindering competition; rather, it is fulfilling its role of defending property rights and protecting against fraud, which could harm producers or consumers. Rothbard also views copyrights as a legitimate property right within a free market economy: when someone purchases a copyrighted work, such as a book, they enter into a contract that prohibits reproduction. Violating this contract constitutes implicit theft, according to Rothbard.

In contrast, Rothbard believes that patents violate free market principles for several reasons. If an invention is patented and another person independently discovers the same innovation, that second inventor cannot utilize their own discovery. This creates a monopolistic privilege for the first inventor that does not apply in the case of copyright. Rothbard argues that patents can only be justified in a capitalist system if they are modeled after copyrights, which he believes should be perpetual rather than time-limited. He contends that any finite duration—such as until the creator's death plus 70 years—would be arbitrary (Rothbard, 1962, pp. 654–657).

More recently, Kinsella (2008 [2001]) revisited Mises' perspective, arguing that patents and copyrights are forms of government monopoly privilege. Unlike Mises, who abstained from taking a clear stance for or against these institutions, Kinsella offers a detailed critique of the common justifications for intellectual property, including utilitarian arguments (like those made by Reisman), contract law arguments (as presented by Rothbard), and natural law arguments (advocated by Ayn Rand's "objectivist" philosophy). From Kinsella's viewpoint, copyright and patent protections constitute state interventions in the market that are both inefficient and unjust. He argues that these laws violate the fundamental libertarian principle of original appropriation, which should govern the appropriation of scarce resources (Hoppe, 1989, p. 17).

9.1.11 Externalities

An externality occurs when the actions of one individual have unintended consequences—known as "external effects"—on another individual. For instance, if my neighbor cultivates beautiful flowerbeds, the enjoyment I derive from admiring this garden constitutes a positive external effect, provided that the garden was not created with the intention of pleasing me. When an externality is beneficial, as in this case, it is termed "positive"; when it is unfavorable, it is referred to as "negative" (for instance, if the neighbor uses their garden as a dumping ground).

The presence of externalities is often used to justify state intervention, based on the argument that if an external effect benefits society, the government should establish a system of incentives to promote actions that generate these positive externalities. Such incentives may include redistributing tax revenues to support activities that yield these benefits. Rothbard (1962, p. 889) critiques this approach, arguing that it forces individuals to pay for services they would not choose to purchase if given the option. While I may enjoy viewing my neighbors' lovely garden, this enjoyment does not warrant a tax imposed on me to compensate them for maintaining their flowerbeds.

Two additional principled challenges can be highlighted (Block, 1996, p. 347). First, positive externalities are so abundant that if the government intervened in each one, it would create a veritable Pandora's box of complications. Block (1983, p. 2) amusingly illustrates this point with the positive externality of wearing socks. Second, the subjectivity of preferences implies that what one person views as a positive externality may be considered a negative externality by another.

One of the primary justifications for state intervention based on positive externalities is public funding of education. Education is believed to generate social benefits that extend beyond the individual knowledge gained, such as reducing crime, fostering social cohesion, promoting civic participation, enhancing democratic engagement, and stimulating economic growth. However, is tax funding for schools and universities—and thus "free" access—justified? West (1994 [1965]) argues negatively and offers a comprehensive critique of the various arguments supporting public funding for education based on positive externalities. In summary, two of his main counterarguments are: (1) education encompasses much more than formal instruction in schools, and (2) there is no reason to assume that families would under-invest in their children's education in the absence of public education services.

9.1.12 The Misesian Critique of Interventionism

The Misesian analysis of price and production control highlights three fundamental characteristics of government interventionism:

- *Impoverishment*: Government intervention tends to lower the average standard of living. While some individuals may prosper and accumulate wealth due to intervention, this occurs at the expense of the majority and results in decreased overall production or a misalignment between supply and demand for goods.
- *Cumulative nature*: Intervention is self-reinforcing; each action generates unintended consequences that necessitate further interventions to address the resulting problems. This cycle can continue indefinitely, leading to an escalation of interventions. Although the government could choose to abandon the initial intervention, if it insists on maintaining it, it will likely have to increase its interventions, which can ultimately lead to complete collectivist control of production, as demonstrated by the history of price controls.
- *Illogical consequences*: Most importantly, interventionism is illogical because it often produces outcomes that are contrary to its intended objectives. For instance, it may cause the very goods that were meant to become more accessible to disappear, lower the standard of living instead of raising it, or induce recessions following credit expansions when the goal was to stimulate production and employment.

Mises places particular emphasis on this illogical aspect because it allows for a purely scientific critique of interventionism, free from value judgments. He concludes (1996 [1929], p. 63) that there is no middle ground between capitalism and collectivism (*tertium non datur*, as the Latin expression goes): either interventions increase and multiply, steering the economic system toward collectivism, or they are dismantled, allowing the system to revert to laissez-faire capitalism. Ikeda (1997) provides a more detailed exploration of this thesis (and see Bylund, 2016 for a recent Austrian analysis of the overall effects of regulation).

9.1.13 Classical Liberalism, Neoliberalism, and Anarcho-Capitalism

The Misesian perspective and its conclusions are closely associated with classical laissez-faire liberalism, characterized by a minimal state or "minarchy." However, the Austrian School also encompasses viewpoints that advocate for anarchism in the sense of a complete rejection of the State, as seen in the works of Rothbard (1977 [1970]) and Hoppe (1989). In contrast, the neoliberal perspective accepts certain state interventions aimed at improving market functioning or addressing perceived shortcomings. For example, Hayek (1944) supports a series of regulations across various domains, including labor (such as mandatory limits on working hours), welfare (guaranteeing a minimum subsistence level for all), insurance (providing public assistance against natural disaster risks), and both monetary and competition policies. Critical examinations and rejections of this Hayekian interventionism are presented by Hoppe (1994) and Block (1996).

Mises occupies a middle ground between pro-capitalist anarchists, who oppose the existence of the State, and neoliberals, who argue that a certain number of government interventions are necessary for the market to function properly (Hülsmann, 2007, p. 708, p. 857).

9.2 Government Taxes and Spending

9.2.1 The Nature of Government Revenue and Spending

Government revenue primarily comes from four sources: taxation, borrowing, production, and inflation (through the central bank). This section will focus on taxation, which is generally the most significant source of government revenue. Taxation involves the *compulsory extraction* of wealth from the population, although, in very rare instances, tax payments may be voluntary. The revenue generated from taxes is then utilized by the

State either as grants or through exchanges. Grants or subsidies are forms of donation, while exchanges refer to payments for labor services (such as civil servants' salaries) or purchases of goods produced by private companies (e.g., military aircrafts).

In all these scenarios, government spending is classified as ***consumption spending***, not investment spending. Monetary expenditures are considered investments only when they are made with the expectation of producing a good whose sale will recoup the initial costs (along with interest). Conversely, expenditures are regarded as consumption when they are used to acquire goods that will not be resold or for which the sale is not anticipated to cover production costs. For instance, public spending on civil servants' salaries or the construction of public infrastructure (such as roads, schools, and hospitals) qualifies as consumption spending. From this perspective, the government functions not as an investor but as a consumer (Rothbard, 1977 [1970], p. 86; Reisman, 1996, p. 446, p. 454).

Austrian economists stand in stark contrast to the Keynesian tradition that promotes "public investment." They align more closely with Classical economic principles. Classical economists differentiated between "productive consumption" (investment), which aims to reproduce wealth with a profit to offset the wealth destroyed in production, and "unproductive consumption," which entails an irreversible and non-reproductive loss of wealth. James Mill (1826 [1821], p. 246) clearly articulated that the government is an unproductive consumer—not because activities like policing and administering justice are without value, but because its spending does not replenish the wealth it consumes. The government can only sustain its operations by reclaiming wealth produced by other economic agents through compulsory taxation.

9.2.2 *Taxes and Redistribution*

Taxes and government payments have significant implications for the production structure. Typically, taxes are imposed at various points in the economic system and then spent on a diverse range of items. However, to grasp the effects of taxation more clearly, it can be helpful to examine a simplified scenario where the tax levy and expenditure are closely linked.

Imagine the government imposes a new tax on a specific sector producing a consumer good, *A*, and then uses that revenue to purchase goods from a different sector, *B* (Rothbard, 1977 [1970], p. 85). This tax increases production costs for firms in sector *A*, leading to a decrease in their profitability. Conversely, the additional income received by firms in sector *B* boosts the demand for their products, raises their selling prices, and enhances their profitability. Consequently, capital is reallocated from sector *A* to sector *B*. Investment and production in sector *A* decline (weaker firms may go bankrupt, and stronger ones may scale back), while investment and production in sector *B* increase (firms expand, and new ones emerge).

The effects ripple through the production structure: firms and sectors upstream of *A* tend to contract, while those upstream of *B* tend to grow. Specific factors of production experience income losses in sector *A* and gains in sector *B*. Non-specific factors, particularly labor, are generally reallocated from sector *A* to sector *B*. Ultimately, sector *A* and its associated supply chain suffer from the tax and contract, while sector *B* and its supply chain benefit from the tax and expand. This dynamic mirrors the changes caused by shifts in consumer preferences, as previously discussed (see Sect. 3.2.13), and reinforces the notion of the State as a consumer. Similar consequences occur when the individuals from whom the tax is collected have different spending profiles compared to those who receive the tax funds.

Two key characteristics of taxation are clearly illustrated here:

1. Taxation *redistributes* wealth in a complex manner, creating a distinction between "taxpayers," who experience a short- or long-term decrease in income, and "tax beneficiaries," who see an increase in their income.
2. Taxes are *never neutral*; they invariably distort the production structure by promoting certain sectors or firms at the expense of others.

9.2.3 Types of Taxes

Rothbard (1977 [1970]) offers a detailed analysis of the various types of taxes and their implications. In a monetary economy, taxes can be assessed based on:

- cash income,
- monetary expenditure,
- capital (i.e., capital values measured in currency).

The primary types of taxes include those levied on gross retail income, various forms of net income (such as wages, rents, interest, and profits/losses), and individual capital.

9.2.4 *The Retail Sales Tax*

Let us consider a scenario in which the government introduces a new tax that takes 5% of all retail sales revenue, using the funds to build and maintain public buildings. Will companies pass this 5% tax on to their sales prices and, consequently, to consumers in the form of higher prices? The answer is no. Companies have already set their selling prices at a level that maximizes their net income, and any increase or decrease in price would reduce their overall revenue. Therefore, it is not in their best interest to change their selling prices. If it had been beneficial for them to raise prices, they would have done so prior to the introduction of the tax. As a result, companies subject to this tax cannot pass it on to consumers. Instead, they will absorb the tax in the income they pay to various economic agents, such as workers, landowners, capitalists, and entrepreneurs, as well as upstream capitalists from whom they purchase capital goods. This scenario exemplifies Rothbard's *incidence rule* (1977 [1970], p. 88): a tax cannot be transferred downstream within the production structure.

During the transitional phase when the new tax takes effect, capitalists may experience capital losses, while branches benefiting from the redistribution may see gains. However, if we disregard this temporary phenomenon, which pertains to profits and losses, and simplify by assuming that the interest rate remains unaffected, it becomes clear that the tax will ultimately be borne by the owners of the original factors of labor and land. This is because the reduction in prices for capital goods ultimately impacts wages and rents. The retail tax essentially acts as an *income tax*. Thus, while the prices of consumer goods may not change significantly on average, overall wages and rents will decline by the amount of the tax.

It is also important to consider that the amount collected by the tax is spent by the State, in this example on the construction of public buildings. This consumption expenditure replaces what would have been spent by taxed workers and landowners. It causes an increase in prices within the public works sector, which then spreads upstream, affecting income derived from the original factors of labor and land. The decrease in wages and rents in the taxed sectors, along with the increase in the beneficiary sector, prompts a reallocation of convertible factors from the former to the latter. Specific original factors, by their very nature, are immobile and experience an increase in income in the beneficiary sector and a decline in the taxed sectors.

For example, a 5% tax on retail sales will not necessarily result in an exact 5% reduction in rents and wages. Some original incomes may be impacted disproportionately, while others may increase due to the reconfiguration of the production structure. Governments often implement retail sales taxes to target consumption; however, in reality, they are taxing—and subsidizing—the incomes of factor owners at varying rates that can differ significantly from the initial 5%.

9.2.5 *The Income Tax*

In a market economy, net income can be categorized into four types: wages, rents, interest, and profits. A tax imposed on these forms of income cannot be transferred upstream in the production structure; thus, it is ultimately borne by workers, landowners, capitalists, and entrepreneurs. By reducing the income associated with these activities, an income tax tends to discourage labor, rental of land, savings, and entrepreneurship among taxpayers. In the (rare) case where the labor supply of taxed individuals is decreasing with wage, they may respond to a decline in income by working more, sacrificing leisure time in the process.

Two additional general effects of income tax can be noted. First, it discriminates against monetary activities in favor of those compensated in kind, since only monetary income is subject to taxation. Second, it encourages individuals to underreport their earnings, as only income declared to the State is taxed.

9.2.6 *The Capital Tax*

Let us consider a scenario in which the government imposes an annual capital tax of 1%. The effect of this tax would be to lower the interest earned on invested capital, which would discourage savings, reduce investment, and ultimately lead to a decline in overall production. Consumer satisfaction would be negatively impacted not only by this reduction in production but also because this type of tax distorts the composition of production. Specifically, the more capital-intensive a sector is—meaning the higher its rate of capital investment—the more that investment will be taxed and subsequently discouraged (Rothbard, 1977 [1970], p. 116).

9.2.7 Tax Level and Progressivity

Taxes result in a redistribution of income and a restructuring of the production landscape, effects that become more pronounced as tax rates increase. Another important consideration is the distribution of the tax burden among taxpayers across different income brackets. This leads to the classic debate between proportional and progressive taxation.

When a tax is highly progressive—meaning it imposes very high rates, such as 75% on the highest income bracket—its primary objective is income equalization. Statistical studies consistently reveal that, due to the small number of taxpayers affected, the revenue generated from such high rates is often negligible as a percentage of total tax revenues (Hayek, 1960, p. 312). A strongly progressive tax is designed to promote egalitarian policies rather than to enhance state revenues. However, it can lead to several adverse effects, as outlined by Hayek (1960, p. 317, p. 320):

- *Disincentive effect*: In a competitive market economy, monetary income reflects the value consumers place on specific activities (imputation principle). A highly disproportionate tax on high incomes discourages individuals from pursuing the most valued economic activities.
- *Resource diversion*: A progressive tax not only reduces overall economic activity but also shifts individuals away from more productive pursuits—where they face higher taxes—toward less productive activities that are taxed at lower rates.
- *Reduction in certain investments*: Long-term investments with the potential for substantial short-term returns may face disproportionately high taxes compared to those with more evenly distributed income over time. For instance, inventors and artists often experience "lean years" before achieving significant success for a few years only. Similarly, high-risk investments that can yield exceptional returns will face challenges due to heavier taxation, unlike safer, less profitable investments.
- *Disruption of the division of labor*: If a worker earns a substantial income and faces a high percentage of tax, they may no longer be able to afford to hire others for simpler tasks. Unless there is a significant income gap, they may need to perform these tasks themselves instead of focusing entirely on their primary, high-productivity work.

- *Restricted capital formation and competition*: Economic progress primarily arises from the implementation of technical or organizational innovations, which often generate high initial revenues. The new capital needed for these innovations is typically sourced from reinvested profits. However, if these revenues are heavily taxed, obtaining the necessary capital becomes more challenging and time-consuming. This not only slows productive innovation but also grants established companies quasi-monopolistic advantages over newer, more productive entrants into the market (Mises, 1998c [1949], p. 805).

9.2.8 State Subsidies

Subsidies represent a first form of government expenditure. Like other forms of state spending, they create a division in society between two groups: recipients and payers. Some individuals receive resources through *political means*, such as confiscation, rather than through *economic means*, that is, voluntary production and exchange (Oppenheimer, 1914). Favoring in this way non-producers over producers tends to expand the group of recipients at the expense of the group of producers. Rothbard (1977 [1970], p. 172) illustrates this point with examples of social benefits, unemployment benefits, and family benefits, which serve as subsidies for poverty, inactivity, and procreation, respectively. Consequently, overall production declines, even when the intention behind the subsidies is to support private firms. In reality, these transfers often benefit struggling companies and result in the preservation of production factors that would otherwise be redirected to more productive uses.

9.2.9 State Services

A second type of government expenditure is dedicated to funding public agencies that provide various services to the population, such as protection (police, military, fire department), education (public schools), healthcare (public hospitals), infrastructure (roads), public transport, mail delivery, and utilities like water and electricity. However, public organizations are often plagued by inefficiency and chronic deficits, which are inevitable consequences of their state-controlled nature (Mises, 1944, p. 45 ff; Rothbard, 1977 [1970], p. 173 ff).

One might wonder why state-run entities are typically less efficient than private enterprises. Could we not simply adopt management practices from private companies to improve state organizations? Unfortunately, this approach is impractical. Even when state services require payment, these public enterprises can always access government funds raised through taxation, while private companies must generate sufficient returns to attract profit-seeking investors. The ability to obtain funding through coercive means rather than voluntary exchange leads to several negative consequences for efficiency: it diminishes incentives for effort and innovation and deprioritizes concerns about budget deficits and user satisfaction. This results in standardized service offerings that often fail to meet the diverse preferences of individuals.

State-owned companies frequently enjoy legal monopolies, which exacerbate these issues. Even in cases where there is competition, they can afford to set prices below cost, effectively eliminating much of the competition from private firms and granting them a de facto monopoly. Furthermore, with low or even zero prices (where services appear "free" since users do not directly pay for them), demand tends to exceed supply, leading to queuing and rationing problems characteristic of markets with price controls (see Sect. 9.1.3).

State-run organizations face a more fundamental challenge: their inability to make economic calculations, which impedes rational resource allocation. A private company survives if its profitability is sufficient to attract investors. This means that the prices customers are willing to pay must cover production costs while also providing a margin to compensate for the capital invested. Economic calculations enable businesses to determine current profits and forecast future profits, helping them decide whether to expand, reduce, or eliminate specific branches based on consumer demand.

In contrast, determining the needs of a government entity, such as a police station, is much more challenging. How can we assess the appropriate number of officers required for law enforcement? We must avoid both overstaffing, which wastes resources, and understaffing, which degrades service quality. Furthermore, how should we allocate budgets among the police, schools, and road maintenance? Since these services are free to users and funded by taxation, no economic calculations can be made, leaving the State unable to rationally determine how to distribute public spending across these areas, or even the total amount to be raised in taxes. Under these conditions, public decision-making can only be very approximate.

If civil servants in each department were allowed to determine their own budgets, they would consistently request more funding. Consequently, public arbitration must occur at the highest levels of government, and even then, these decisions are political in nature. They resemble *consumption decisions* made by individuals rather than investment decisions based on the economic calculations of capital and net income.

9.2.10 Minimizing Public Spending

The Austrian theory of interventionism concludes that state intervention in the market has a detrimental effect on economic prosperity. The theories of taxation and public spending arrive at the same conclusion: these government activities distort the structure of production, impede the competitive process, and discourage productive endeavors while politicizing society. In this context, political activism often thrives at the expense of productive capabilities (Hoppe, 1989, p. 55).

From a macroeconomic perspective, government taxes and expenditures tend to:

- *Reduce overall revenue*—especially when spending is directed toward redistribution or funding services that could be provided by the private market.
- *Alter the balance of goods and services* produced compared to what consumers actually desire.
- *Decrease savings and investment* while increasing interest rates, primarily due to public borrowing and taxes imposed on capital and interest income.
- *Diminish the value of money*, especially when government spending is financed through money creation.

According to the principle of *axiological neutrality*, it is impossible to logically derive a political recommendation solely from scientific reasoning. However, it is easy to understand the general opposition among Austrian economists to excessive government spending. The definition of what constitutes "excess" varies according to one's political philosophy: for anarcho-capitalists advocating for the abolition of the State, even minimal expenditure is considered excessive; for minarchists, only spending necessary to maintain a minimal state—such as funding for the police, judiciary, and military—is justified; and for neoliberals, some additional government spending may be seen as desirable (see Sect. 9.1.13).

9.3 Collectivism

9.3.1 The Collectivist State

While capitalism is characterized by private ownership of the factors of production, collectivism is defined by "common" or "collective" ownership of these resources, including farmland, deposits, factories, warehouses, machines, and so on. However, "collective" ownership does not imply that individuals can freely claim and use the factors of production as they wish; such an arrangement would lead to continuous and insurmountable conflict. Instead, it signifies that the utilization of all production factors is entrusted to a single entity—a supreme economic authority we might refer to as the "State." This authority is tasked with organizing and planning production in service of the "common good."

Debates about the nature of this "common good" and the structure of this supreme authority—whether it arises from democratic elections or dictatorial power—are issues of morality and politics, and fall outside the realm of economic analysis (Mises, 1981 [1922], p. 112). Additionally, questions regarding whether workers would have the freedom to choose their occupations or be assigned jobs compulsorily are also set aside in this discussion.

Proponents of collectivism argue that capitalism has two significant flaws: first, it is an "anarchic" system in which producers make independent decisions, leading to destructive competition; second, it merely reflects and even exacerbates individual egoism. In this light, collectivism may seem a superior solution, as it replaces the chaos of production with a coherent government plan and shifts the focus from individual self-interest to objectives defined by a State that supposedly prioritizes the general interest. On the surface, a collectivist regime appears appealing. However, the question remains: can it function effectively? Mises (1935 [1920]) formulated a theory of economic calculation that led him to answer this question in the negative.

9.3.2 The Economic Problem

A developed economic system consists of a multitude of production factors, a vast array of techniques for transforming these factors into final consumer goods, and a diverse range of individual preferences. The fundamental "economic problem" is determining how to utilize these production factors most effectively to satisfy people's needs. In other words, how should these factors be allocated among different production lines to allow individuals to achieve their most important goals? Additionally, how can we minimize the waste of resources by avoiding the production of goods considered less important, especially when more important goods could have been produced instead? In short, the economic problem revolves around allocating scarce resources to alternative uses based on previously determined goals (Robbins, 1932, p. 15).

It is crucial to understand that this problem cannot be solved purely through technical means, except in very simple or unrealistic scenarios. A technical solution might be conceivable if all factors were completely specific or perfectly substitutable for one another (in other words, if there were essentially only one factor of production). However, since many factors are convertible and substitution possibilities are often limited, an economic calculation tool is essential for rationally allocating productive resources.

9.3.3 Economic Calculation and Market Prices

In a capitalist system, economic calculation is facilitated by market prices expressed in monetary terms (see Sect. 7.1.6). These prices allow each producer to evaluate numerically the anticipated profitability of their projects. If this profitability is deemed insufficient, it indicates that the expected sales price does not cover the unit costs, including interest on the invested capital. Why might costs be too high? Typically, this occurs because other producers anticipate a strong enough demand from their customers and compete for the same factors of production, driving up their prices by imputation. All of these calculations hinge on predicted future prices and demand, despite inherent uncertainties. Producers may sometimes realize, after the fact, that their expectations were incorrect. However, this does not undermine the usefulness of the market price system, as it is precisely through this system that producers can make initial decisions, recognize any mistakes they made, and rectify them throughout the market process.

9.3.4 The Impossibility of Economic Calculation Under Collectivism

In a collectivist economic system, the State is, by definition, the sole owner of the factors of production. Even if an exchange system and currency exist, their use is strictly limited to consumer goods. Given the diversity of individual preferences, allowing people to exchange consumer goods is beneficial, as it enhances overall satisfaction through voluntary transactions. However, because factors of production are owned exclusively by the State, they cannot be traded, which would require at least *two* distinct owners. Without the possibility of exchange, there can be no prices for the factors of production, rendering economic calculation *impossible.*

Mises' critique of collectivism is straightforward: it cannot function because it lacks a means of economic calculation. The leaders of a collectivist system are unable to address the fundamental economic problem of rationally allocating production factors to best satisfy the ends they wish to pursue.

Consider, for instance, if the collectivist State decides to build an automobile factory. How can it determine whether the production factors allocated to this factory should instead be used to fulfill other needs deemed more important by people? Why choose to locate the plant in one area over another? What should the factory's size and durability be? Why select one material over another for construction? What method of car manufacturing should be employed? What types of metals or materials should be used for specific vehicle components? While market prices provide rational answers to these questions, the collectivist State, lacking a mechanism for economic calculation, is left to make arbitrary production decisions. Mises concludes that a collectivized system can never achieve the productive efficiency of a capitalist system and may lead to the disintegration of the division of labor and significant impoverishment (1981 [1922], p. 105, p. 117).

9.3.5 Critique of the Historical Argument

The first and most obvious objection to Mises is that collectivist regimes have existed throughout history—and still exist today, albeit in very small numbers. The former Soviet Union serves as the most emblematic example. For these regimes to exist, they must have functioned in some capacity. However, the response to this objection is that Mises' argument regarding economic calculation should be applied rigorously to isolated collectivist regimes. Historically, communist countries have coexisted alongside capitalist ones, allowing them to gain invaluable information about market prices for various goods, particularly natural resources, in global markets. They also had the opportunity to acquire, whether legally or illegally, production techniques and new types of goods from capitalist nations.

Despite this advantageous situation, which somewhat alleviated their economic calculation problems, these collectivist regimes were notoriously dysfunctional. Their production processes were chaotic and, most importantly, insufficient, failing to adequately meet the needs of their populations—even when endowed with significant natural resources, as was the case with the USSR. These serious challenges can be explained through the theory of economic calculation: prices in capitalist countries could never accurately reflect what they would be in collectivized nations. Furthermore, the theory of interventionism posits that universal price controls and extensive wealth redistribution lead to increased rationing and demotivated producers.

9.3.6 Critique of the Marxist Solution

Marx and Engels adhered to the labor theory of value formulated by Classical economists and suggested in some of their writings that a collectivized economy could potentially employ economic calculation based on labor time (Mises, 1935 [1920], p. 112; Lavoie, 1985, p. 68). By knowing the total available labor force and the quantities of labor needed to produce different types of goods, the state could allocate workers to various production tasks.

Mises identifies two insurmountable difficulties with this Marxist solution. First, because it relies exclusively on labor, it overlooks the use of natural resources (factors of production, such as land). For instance, two production processes might require the same amount of labor time but use vastly different quantities of natural resources. This significant difference would not be captured in a calculation based solely on labor hours.

The second difficulty with the Marxist solution lies in its reliance on arbitrary substitution rates between different qualities of labor. An hour of skilled labor is worth more than an hour of unskilled labor, but what is the precise quantitative relationship between the two? In the absence of labor markets, the relationships among the various types of labor are unknown, making it impossible for a central planner to effectively incorporate different kinds of skilled labor into their calculations. Neighboring capitalist countries could provide this information, but proponents of collectivism aim to eliminate capitalism, not maintain it as a kind of data center.

9.3.7 *Critique of the Mathematical Solution*

In the tradition of mathematical economics (Walras, 1874), the equilibrium of the economic system—and the optimal allocation of resources—is conceptualized as the solution to a system of equations, where the unknowns are prices, and the parameters include individual preferences, the available stock of goods, and firms' production techniques. One might wonder why a planner in a collectivist regime could not organize the economy by solving these Walrasian general equilibrium equations. However, according to Hayek (1935, p. 208), such a solution is entirely impractical.

It necessitates that the planning organization has centralized knowledge of (1) all available factors of production, distinguished by their location, condition, and any other attributes affecting their productive capacity (such as the quality and quantity of complementary goods); (2) all production techniques across various fields; and (3) individual preferences for all conceivable consumer goods. This immense amount of information is not only vast but also subject to unpredictable changes at any moment due to local production and consumption conditions. Solving a colossal system of equations, whose parameters are numerous and change faster than they can be communicated to a central computing center, is utterly inconceivable. Thus, the mathematical solution significantly overestimates the computational and informational capabilities of a planning center. This criticism emphasizes that the capitalist system leverages an extraordinary amount of technical knowledge and information, from the most general to the most localized, and that these changes are swiftly addressed by the relevant actors (see Sect. 3.2.14).

Mises' argument (1998c [1949], p. 706 ff) against the mathematical solution differs from Hayek's. Instead of concentrating on the complexity of the problem, as Hayek does, Mises highlights the planner's challenge in determining the path by which the economic system can transition from its present state to the general equilibrium. At the initial moment t_0, the economic system is characterized by a specific endowment of factors of production distributed among various firms. Suppose the planner possesses all the necessary information and can successfully solve the Walrasian general equilibrium equations, thereby knowing the final equilibrium state to be achieved at a future time t_1. However, he remains unaware of how to reach this final equilibrium.

The solution to the general equilibrium equations provides no insight into the process by which the system can transition from its initial state to the target state. Solving the mathematical problem, even if it is theoretically feasible, merely indicates the objective to be attained, not the sequence of steps necessary to accomplish it. In such a case, it is futile to know your destination if you do not know how to reach it.

9.3.8 Critique of the Decentralized Planning System

Calculating in kind is impossible (you cannot mix apples and oranges), and the Marxist approach of measuring in man-hours yields inaccurate results. Additionally, solving the general equilibrium equations is both impractical and futile. This raises the fundamental question: how can the complex issue of economic calculation be addressed?

Starting in the 1930s, Neoclassical economists who supported socialism proposed a new type of collectivism that resembled a capitalist system more closely (Lange, 1936, 1937). Their idea involved implementing "decentralized" planning. In this model, the central authority would provide company managers with a set of prices to guide their economic calculations. Each company would then formulate its production plan based on these prices, aiming to maximize "profit." This process would result in quantities supplied and quantities demanded for each good. These figures would be sent back to the central authority, which would aggregate them to identify market imbalances: if the supply of a good exceeded demand, the central authority would lower its price; conversely, if demand exceeded supply, the price would be raised. The central authority would then send updated prices to the company managers, who would revise their production plans accordingly. This cycle would continue, with the central authority adjusting prices in response to the newly reported quantities supplied and demanded. It is important to note that company directors do not own their firms and cannot appropriate profits; instead, these profits are collected and redistributed by the State.

This proposed solution is paradoxical (Mises, 1998c [1949], p. 702). Originally, collectivism and planning were intended to eliminate capitalist markets and competition. Yet, some Neoclassical economists ended up acknowledging that a form of market pricing is essential, even within a system that claims to be entirely socialist.

Hayek (1948 [1940]) critiques this decentralized planning approach, arguing that while it theoretically addresses the issue of economic calculation, it falls short in practice. It might function effectively in a static equilibrium, where the central authority could make only minor adjustments.

Under such conditions, a trial-and-error method could indeed suffice. However, the reality is that dynamic shocks of various types and magnitudes constantly disrupt the system. While decentralized planning may work in a static environment, it is ill-equipped to handle the complexities and uncertainties of a dynamic, developed economy. This may explain why such methods have never been implemented in practice, despite the extensive theoretical exploration by mainstream Neoclassical economists.

Mises (1981 [1922], p. 105) had already critiqued this solution, highlighting that the problem of economic calculation emerges primarily in a dynamic economy characterized by frequent, unpredictable changes across all sectors. Under the unrealistic assumption of a static economy, a competent collectivist regime might seem feasible. However, under realistic conditions, such a regime will be highly inefficient, regardless of whether it employs centralized or decentralized planning.

9.3.9 "De-Homogenizing" Mises and Hayek?

For Mises, unlike Hayek, the core issue with collectivism is not merely one of information but fundamentally revolves around economic calculation. This is essentially a problem of *property rights*, as property rights give rise to exchange, which in turn generates prices that make possible economic calculation. Without private property rights in the factors of production, economic calculation becomes impossible. As previously discussed, Mises argues that even if the planning center possesses perfect information—knowing all preferences, techniques, and available factors—it still cannot implement rational decision-making without a means of calculation. In such a scenario, the Center would be unable to efficiently allocate the resources at its disposal to achieve its intended objectives.

On the other hand, Hayek emphasizes that the primary challenge in a collectivist regime lies in the *dissemination* of knowledge and information throughout the economic system. He posits that if the planner could successfully centralize this dispersed information, an effective plan could be devised and executed. However, the task of centralization is impractical, preventing a collectivist regime from harnessing the extensive knowledge and information needed by a complex economic system.

According to the "de-homogenization" thesis, Mises and Hayek have developed fundamentally different critiques of collectivism, addressing distinct issues: property rights for Mises and information dissemination for

Hayek. This thesis is, however, contentious. It is supported by scholars such as Salerno (1990, 1993), Hoppe (1996), and Hülsmann (1997), while others, including Kirzner (1996) and Yeager (1997), argue that Hayek's critique is, in fact, an extension of Mises' arguments.

9.3.10 *The Austrian Perspective on the Debate*

The original article by Mises (1935 [1920]) sparked a vigorous and extensive debate on the feasibility of collectivism. Boettke (2000) has compiled the key texts from this discussion into a nine-volume collection! However, the narrative of this debate varies significantly depending on whether one adopts a standard Neoclassical or an Austrian perspective (Lavoie, 1985).

From the standard Neoclassical viewpoint, the Austrians quickly lost the debate to the Neoclassical arguments. Mises asserted that economic calculation was "impossible" under a collectivist regime. Yet, with the introduction of a decentralized planning system, proponents claimed that such calculations are theoretically feasible, effectively concluding the debate in favor of Neoclassical economists.

The Austrian interpretation presents a fundamentally different narrative. Standard Neoclassical economists have misunderstood the essence of Mises' argument because they operate within a framework heavily influenced by the concept of equilibrium. However, economic reality never aligns with the notion of final equilibrium; this concept serves merely as a theoretical construct that allows for a better understanding of the market process, which is inherently characterized by multiple imbalances, varying degrees of profit and loss at different points in the system, and the critical role of entrepreneurship.

Thus, the real issue is not whether economic calculation is possible "in principle" within a collectivist regime, but whether a collectivist planner would have access to a reliable and precise tool for economic calculation in practice. The decentralized planning method relies on a static and therefore insufficient representation of the economic order, failing to address the Misesian argument effectively. Consequently, the Austrians were not defeated but rather misinterpreted by their Neoclassical counterparts.

The critique of collectivism thus enhances the Austrian critique of interventionism: state intervention not only reduces the average standard of living but also, through its cumulative effects, gradually steers the economic system toward a dysfunctional collectivist regime. This chapter, along with the previous one, illustrates that Austrian liberalism or libertarianism is grounded not in ideology but in scientific analysis. Their *scientific theories* demonstrate that it is the State—rather than the free market—that is responsible for inflation, economic crises, mass unemployment, and significant monopolistic restrictions.

References

Armentano, D. T. (1996 [1982]). *Antitrust and Monopoly: Anatomy of a Policy Failure* (2nd ed.). The Independent Institute.

Block, W. (1983). Public Goods and Externalities: The Case of Roads. *Journal of Libertarian Studies, 7*(1), 1–34.

Block, W. (1996). Hayek's Road to Serfdom. *Journal of Libertarian Studies, 12*(2), 339–365.

Boettke, P. (Ed.). (2000). *Socialism and the Market: The Socialist Calculation Debate Revisited*. Routledge.

Bylund, P. L. (2016). *The Seen, the Unseen, and the Unrealized: How Regulations Affect Our Everyday Lives*. Lexington Books.

Hayek, F. A. (1935). The Present State of the Debate. In F. A. Hayek (Ed.), *Collectivist Economic Planning: Critical Studies on the Possibilities of Socialism* (pp. 201–243). George Routledge and Sons.

Hayek, F. A. (1944). *The Road to Serfdom*. The University of Chicago Press.

Hayek, F. A. (1948 [1940]). The Competitive "Solution". In F. A. Hayek (Ed.), *Individualism and Economic Order* (pp. 181–208). The University of Chicago Press.

Hayek, F. A. (1960). *The Constitution of Liberty*. Routledge & Kegan Paul.

Hayek, F. A. (1967 [1959]). Unions, Inflation and Profits. In F. A. Hayek (Ed.), *Studies in Philosophy, Politics and Economics* (pp. 280–294). Routledge & Kegan Paul.

Hoppe, H.-H. (1989). *A Theory of Socialism and Capitalism: Economics, Politics, and Ethics*. Kluwer.

Hoppe, H.-H. (1994). FA Hayek on Government and Social Evolution: A Critique. *Review of Austrian Economics, 7*(1), 67–93.

Hoppe, H.-H. (1996). Socialism: A Property or Knowledge Problem? *Review of Austrian Economics, 9*(1), 143–149.

Hülsmann, J. G. (1997). Knowledge, Judgment, and the Use of Property. *Review of Austrian Economics, 10*(1), 23–48.

Hülsmann, J. G. (2007). *Mises: The Last Knight of Liberalism*. Ludwig von Mises Institute.

Ikeda, S. (1997). *Dynamics of the Mixed Economy: Toward a Theory of Interventionism*. Routledge.

Kinsella, S. N. (2008 [2001]). *Against Intellectual Property.* Ludwig von Mises Institute.
Kirzner, I. M. (1996). Reflections on the Misesian Legacy in Economics. *Review of Austrian Economics, 9*(2), 143–154.
Lange, O. (1936). On the Economic Theory of Socialism. *Review of Economic Studies, 4*, 53–71.
Lange, O. (1937). On the Economic Theory of Socialism. *Review of Economic Studies, 5*, 132–142.
Lavoie, D. (1982). The Development of the Misesian Theory of Interventionism. In I. M. Kirzner (Ed.), *Method, Process, and Austrian Economics: Essays in Honor of Ludwig Von Mises* (pp. 169–183). Lexington Books.
Lavoie, D. (1985). *Rivalry and Central Planning: The Socialist Calculation Debate Reconsidered.* Cambridge University Press.
Mill, J. (1826 [1821]). *Elements of Political Economy* (3rd ed.). Baldwin and Cradock.
Oppenheimer, F. (1914). *The State.* Vanguard Press.
Reisman, G. (1996). *Capitalism: A Treatise on Economics.* Jameson Books.
Robbins, L. (1932). *An Essay on the Nature and Significance of Economic Science.* Macmillan.
Rothbard, M. N. (1962). *Man, Economy, and State: A Treatise on Economic Principles.* D. Van Nostrand.
Rothbard, M. N. (1977 [1970]). *Power and Market: Government and the Economy.* Sheed Andrews and McMeel.
Rothbard, M. N. (1998 [1982]). *The Ethics of Liberty.* New York University Press.
Salerno, J. T. (1990). Ludwig Von Mises as Social Rationalist. *Review of Austrian Economics, 4*, 26–54.
Salerno, J. T. (1993). Mises and Hayek Dehomogenized. *Review of Austrian Economics, 6*(2), 113–146.
Thornton, M. (1991). *The Economics of Prohibition.* University of Utah Press.
von Mises, L. (1923). Theory of Price Controls. In L. Von Mises (1996 [1929]) (pp. 97–106).
von Mises, L. (1926). Interventionism. In L. Von Mises (1996 [1929]), (pp. 1–31).
von Mises, L. (1935 [1920]). Economic Calculation in the Socialist Commonwealth. In F. A. Hayek (Ed.), *Collectivist Economic Planning: Critical Studies on the Possibilities of Socialism* (pp. 87–130). George Routledge & Sons.
von Mises, L. (1944). *Bureaucracy.* Yale University Press.
von Mises, L. (1981 [1922]). *Socialism: An Economic and Sociological Analysis.* Liberty Classics.
von Mises, L. (1996 [1929]). *Critique of Interventionism.* The Foundation for Economic Education.
von Mises, L. (1998a [1940]). *Interventionism: An Economic Analysis.* The Foundation for Economic Education.

von Mises, L. (1998b [1944]). Monopoly Prices. *Quarterly Journal of Austrian Economics, 1*(2), 1–28.
von Mises, L. (1998c [1949]). *Human Action: A Treatise on Economics.* Ludwig von Mises Institute.
Walras, L. (1874). *Éléments d'Économie Politique Pure.* Corbaz.
West, E. G. (1994 [1965]). *Education and the State: A Study in Political Economy.* Liberty Fund.
Yeager, L. B. (1997). Calculation and Knowledge: Let's Write *Finis. Review of Austrian Economics, 10*(1), 133–136.

CHAPTER 10

Conclusion

Abstract The Austrian School's integrated approach to economic analysis links value, price, interest, money, production, and business cycles into a cohesive system, emphasizing dynamic, entrepreneurial competition as central to understanding market processes. Standard Neoclassical economics is criticized for its reliance on partial and general equilibrium models that neglect real-world price formation. Austrian economics rejects the micro-macro divide and offers a consistent, sound, and comprehensive non-mathematical alternative to fragmented and over-formalized mainstream theories.

Keywords Market process • Unified micro- and macroeconomics

A defining characteristic of the Austrian School is its integrated system of economic analysis. Its value theory naturally develops into theories of prices, interest (or capitalization), and money, which then form the basis for theories on production structure, economic progress, and business cycles. This intellectual framework, gradually established by Menger, Böhm-Bawerk, and Fetter, and later expanded by Mises and Hayek, maintains coherence as each contribution builds upon the last. While there is some divergence in views on the origin of interest—subjectivity for Fetter

R. Fillieule, *The Austrian School of Economics*, Palgrave Studies in Austrian Economics,
https://doi.org/10.1007/978-3-031-83414-1_10

and Mises, and productivity for Böhm-Bawerk and Hayek—this difference results from two interpretations of the same theoretical framework. Figure 10.1 illustrates how these elements are organized, according to Mises' interpretation.

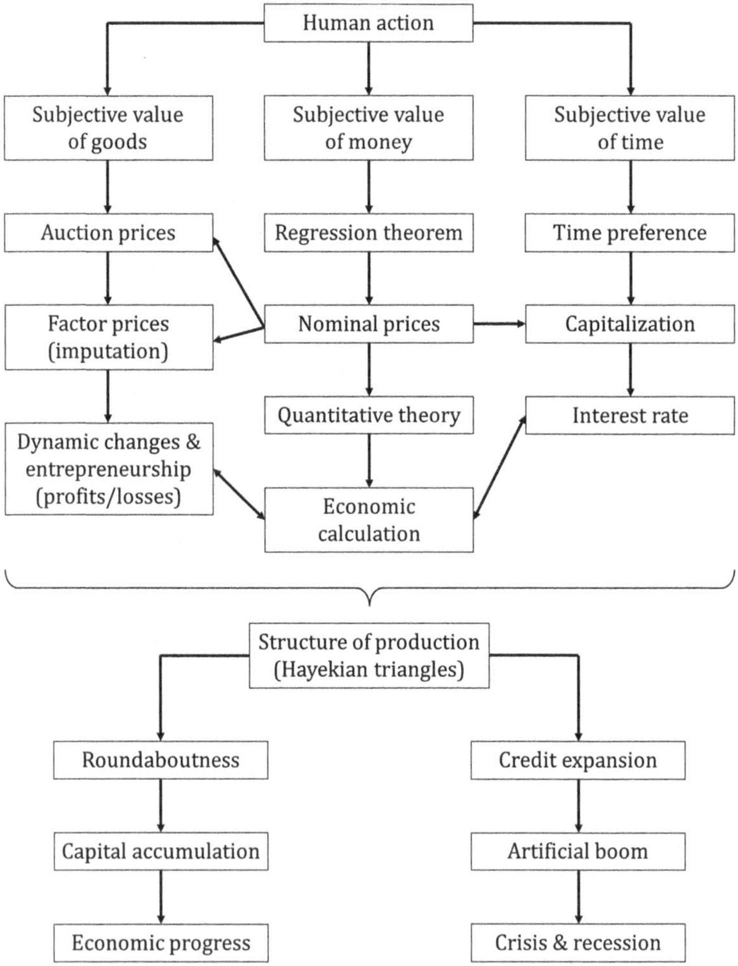

Fig. 10.1 An integrated system of economic analysis

The contrast with the standard Neoclassical School is stark. In the Neoclassical framework found in any textbook today, economic science is presented in a fragmented way. There is a sharp division between microeconomics, which centers on models of perfect and monopolistic competition, and macroeconomics, which primarily addresses growth—with no theoretical link bridging these two aspects. The Austrian School rejects this rigid separation between competition theory and growth theory. For Austrians, entrepreneurial competition involves reallocating resources from less productive uses to more productive ones, while growth is simply the aggregate outcome of these reallocations across markets. While one might distinguish between a "micro" perspective focused on competition and a "macro" perspective centered on growth (or "economic progress," as Mises terms it), these aspects are so closely interconnected that neither can be fully understood in isolation.

Standard micro- and macroeconomic domains are also further divided internally. For instance, "orthodox" microeconomics is split between partial and general equilibrium models—a distinction that not only does not exist in the Austrian School but is also seen as a significant theoretical flaw.

Reasoning in terms of partial equilibrium means, on the one hand, disregarding the external influence of factors outside the market being analyzed and, on the other, treating these external forces as fixed data or parameters. From the Austrian perspective, this approach is not a scientifically valid simplification but a fundamental error in reasoning. Since its founding by Menger, the Austrian paradigm emphasizes imputation, a process by which anticipated product values and prices shape the values and prices of the factors used in their production. Böhm-Bawerk's reinterpretation of the "law of costs" further illustrates these upward connections, which are entirely overlooked in partial equilibrium models, highlighting the necessity of analyzing interconnected markets.

In examining how an economic system adapts to dynamic shocks, such as changes in demand or techniques, we observe how these shifts generate profits in some markets, balanced by losses in others. These profits and losses cascade across markets, impacting the entire economy and leading to a reallocation of original production factors. Thinking in terms of "partial equilibrium" entirely misses this causal chain of analysis, obscuring our understanding of the essential mechanisms of the price system and the market economy.

From this perspective, general equilibrium models might appear more satisfying since they consider the broad interdependence between markets.

However, they, too, have serious limitations. First, they only explain equilibrium prices, whereas real-world market prices, shaped by entrepreneurial competition, are not equilibrium prices. These prices often coexist with market imbalances, such as profits, losses, shortages, or unsold goods. Second, the general equilibrium model's approach to price determination is highly debatable: it treats equilibrium prices as unknowns in a set of mathematical equations, to be determined simultaneously as solutions to this system. This approach overlooks how entrepreneurial dynamics influence the final equilibrium state.

The Austrian analysis, with its focus on the causal chain following dynamic shocks, enables a study of real market price formation while avoiding the flawed metaphor of simultaneous equations—since, in reality, prices do not reach equilibrium all at once. Finally, general equilibrium models exclude money, relying instead on a barter system. By contrast, the Austrian School, through Mises' regression theorem, enables an analysis of market interdependence that includes monetary prices. Thus, Austrian theory not only sidesteps the limitations of both partial and general equilibrium models but also unifies price theory and monetary theory.

Standard macroeconomics is divided between a largely "Keynesian" short-term approach (featuring money non-neutrality and liquidity preference) and a more "classical" long-term perspective (assuming money neutrality and the quantitative theory of money). This split between short- and long-term analysis is one of macroeconomics' main weaknesses. The problem here is clear: when does the short-term transition into the long term, and at what point should Keynesian principles give way to Classical ones? From an Austrian viewpoint, these questions are meaningless. Each successive period remains short term, requiring the same explanatory principles as those applied in the previous short-term period.

This twofold problem of standard macroeconomics—having contradictory reasoning principles depending on the context (Keynesian vs. Classical) and an unsatisfactory linkage between short- and long-term views—does not exist in the Austrian paradigm. For Mises, the long term is not a future real-world period but a theoretical construct, a hypothetical state where the economy has fully adjusted to an initial shock, with no further disturbances (under the condition of "all else being equal"). The long term, therefore, serves purely as a conceptual tool to analyze the ultimate effects of a dynamic change, not as a state that will materialize in the real world. In this framework, it is nonsensical to suggest that money is non-neutral in the short term and neutral in the long term, since, in the long term, the system is in a static equilibrium where money no longer plays a role. Nor does it make sense to shift reasoning principles between the short and long term, as the long term is merely the cumulative outcome of successive short-term periods. The same principles of analysis apply throughout—using time preference (or capital productivity) to explain the interest rate and the quantity theory of money to explain purchasing power.

While the standard Neoclassical paradigm is split into loosely connected, often contradictory sub-fields, the Austrian School has developed, over generations—and particularly through Mises' synthesis in his treatise *Human Action*—a cohesive and comprehensive system of economic understanding derived from a few foundational principles. We hope this short book has helped readers appreciate this integrative and verbal approach, which differs significantly from more conventional theories that rely on inconsistent perspectives and mathematical formalism.

Index

R. Fillieule, *The Austrian School of Economics*, Palgrave Studies in Austrian Economics,
https://doi.org/10.1007/978-3-031-83414-1

The manufacturer's authorised representative in the EU is Springer
Nature Customer Service Centre GmbH, Europaplatz 3, 69115 Heidelberg,
Germany. If you have any concerns regarding our products, please
contact ProductSafety@springernature.com

Printed and bound by CPI Group (UK) Ltd, Croydon, CR0 4YY
01/10/2026
02225924-0002